Pocket Rough Guide

AMSTERDAM

written and researched by

PHIL LEE

Contents

<< KEIZERSGRACHT
< EYE FILM INSTITUTE

INTRODUCTION TO Amsterdam

Amsterdam is simply unique. You could be sitting nursing a drink outside one of its cafés, chugging along its canals by boat, or riding its cheerful trams, and you'll know immediately that you couldn't be anywhere else in the world. What is it that makes the place so exceptional? Well, its watery cityscape means that much of the centre is off-limits to traffic; its architecture is for the most part on a human rather than a grandiose scale; and its people are a welcoming bunch on the whole, proud of their city but not stuck in the past. Amsterdam is always changing but has an uncanny – and reassuring – ability to stay much the same as it has always been.

FLOWER MARKET BY THE SINGEL CANAL

BROUWERSGRACHT

In part it's the liberal traditions of the city that have given Amsterdam its distinctive character, beginning with the obvious legalized prostitution and dope-smoking coffeeshops. More subtle qualities are encapsulated by Amsterdammers themselves in the word *gezellig*, a very Dutch concept which roughly corresponds to "warmly convivial" – something perhaps most manifest in the city's wonderfully diverse selection of bars and cafés. Amsterdam is also riding something of a resurgent wave, with dozens of great new restaurants, a vibrant arts life and a club scene that has come of age. As if this wasn't enough, there's also the reinvention of neighbourhoods like De Pijp and the ambitious redevelopment of the old docklands bordering the River IJ, featuring glittering new public buildings such as the EYE film institute (see p.96) and the library (see p.93).

All that said, the Old Centre remains the commercial heart of the city. Spreading south from Centraal Station, and including Amsterdam's notorious Red Light District, the district's narrow canals are bordered by old merchants' houses and a jangle of newer buildings. Moving on, the layout of the rest of the city centre is determined by a web of canals that loop right round the centre as the so-called

Best places for...a cold beer in summer

It's hard to imagine a more chilled-out place than Amsterdam in summer. Here are some of our favourite spots to kick back with an alfresco *vaasje* (glass of beer): > **Het Papeneiland p.69** > **Proust p.79** > **De Sluyswacht p.89** > **Gent aan de Schinkel p.107** > **In de Wildeman p.51**

AMSTERDAM AT NIGHT

When to visit

Amsterdam has warm, mild summers and moderately cold and wet winters. The climate is certainly not severe enough to make much difference to the city's routines, which makes Amsterdam an ideal all-year destination. That said, high summer – roughly late June to August – sees the city's parks packed to the gunnels and parts of the centre almost overwhelmed by tourists. Spring and autumn are not too crowded and can be especially beautiful, with mist hanging over the canals and low sunlight beaming through the cloud cover. Even in January and February, when the light can be at its gloomiest, there are compensations – wet cobbles glistening under the street lights and the canals rippled by falling raindrops. In the summer, from around June to August, mosquitoes can be bothersome.

Grachtengordel, a planned, seventeenth-century extension to the medieval town, with its tall, elegant gabled houses reflected in olive-green waters.

There are plenty of first-rate attractions, most notably the Anne Frank Huis, the Rijksmuseum, with its wonderful collection of Dutch paintings, the peerless Van Gogh Museum and the newly renovated Stedelijk gallery of modern art. But it's not all about the sights: Amsterdam is a great city just to be in, with no attractions so important that they have to interrupt lazy days of wandering the canals and taking in the city at your own pace. Finally, don't forget that the Netherlands is a small country and there are plenty of compelling attractions close by, not least the small town of Haarlem, with the great Frans Hals Museum, the Zuider Zee villages to the north, and the stunning Keukenhof Gardens – all very easy to reach by public transport.

AMSTERDAM AT A GLANCE

>> EATING

The **food** in the average Dutch restaurant has improved hugely in recent years, and there are many places serving inventive takes on homegrown cuisine. The city also has a good assortment of ethnic restaurants, especially Indonesian, Chinese and Thai. There are lots of bars – known as *eetcafés* – that serve adventurous food for a decent price in a relaxed and unpretentious setting. Note that the Dutch eat out relatively early, with most restaurants opening at 5.30pm or 6pm and closing around 10pm.

>> COFFEESHOPS

Although the city plans to close down a number of places over the next few years, Amsterdam continues to be known for its **coffeeshops**, which are permitted to sell small quantities of **cannabis** and ready-made joints. The majority of coffeeshops are found in the Old Centre and generally look like regular cafés. Prevented from advertising (you need to look at a menu to see what's on offer) they usually sell a wide range of Dutch weed, grown under artificial lights, as well as compressed resin such as *Pollem*. Most of it is extremely potent and to be handled with care – ask before you buy to avoid any unpleasant surprises. Coffeeshops usually open at 10am or 11am and close around midnight.

>> SHOPPING

The **Nieuwendijk/Kalverstraat** strip in the Old Centre is home to high-street fashion and mainstream department stores, while nearby **Koningsplein** and **Leidsestraat** offer designer clothes and shoe stores. You'll find more offbeat clothes shops in the Jordaan and in the small radial streets that connect the main canals of the Grachtengordel – an area known as the Nine Streets. The cream of Amsterdam's antique trade is in the Spiegelkwartier, centred on **Nieuwe Spiegelstraat**. As regards **opening hours**, many shops take Monday morning off; Thursday is late-opening night, with most places staying open until 9pm.

>> DRINKING & NIGHTLIFE

Amsterdam's selection of bars range from traditional **brown cafés** – cosy places so called because of the dingy colour of their walls, stained by years of tobacco smoke – to slick **designer bars**. Most places stay open until around midnight or 1am during the week, and until 2am at weekends. Look out for the few **tasting houses** or *proeflokalen* that are left, originally the sampling rooms of small private distillers, now tiny, stand-up places specializing in *jenever* (gin); they tend to close around 8pm. The **clubbing** scene is first-rate, and there are lots of bars with DJs, as well as an array of live music options, particularly for jazz.

OUR RECOMMENDATIONS FOR WHERE TO EAT, DRINK AND SHOP ARE LISTED AT THE END OF EACH PLACES CHAPTER.

Day One in Amsterdam

1 The Dam > p.36. The heart of the city, and what better place to start?

2 Koninklijk Paleis > p.37. The confidence and pride of the Golden Age – in a building.

3 Nieuwe Kerk > p.38. No longer used as a church, but still one of the city's most impressive Gothic buildings.

4 Nine Streets > p.58. These streets connecting the main canals are the epitome of what makes Amsterdam special – full of intriguing one-off shops and cafés.

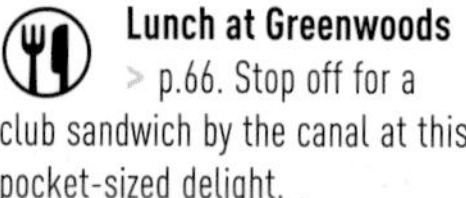

Lunch at Greenwoods > p.66. Stop off for a club sandwich by the canal at this pocket-sized delight.

5 The Grachtengordel > pp.52–71. After shopping, just get lost in the web of stately seventeenth-century canals that make Amsterdam so unique.

6 Westerkerk > p.57. Rembrandt's burial place, and the city's grandest Reformation-era landmark.

7 Anne Frank Huis > p.57. The city's most renowned – and moving – sight, bar none.

8 The Jordaan > p.72. One of Amsterdam's most wanderable and picturesque districts, full of independent stores, bars and restaurants.

Dinner at Moeders > p.77. There's no better place to wind up of an evening than at this big, lively and very authentic Dutch restaurant on the edge of the Jordaan.

Day Two in Amsterdam

1 Rijksmuseum > p.101. One of Europe's finest museums with a magnificent collection of Rembrandts.

2 Van Gogh Museum > p.103. The greatest collection of the prolific nineteenth-century artist's work by far, and with good temporary exhibits too.

Lunch at Café Loetje > p.107. Lunch on the best steaks and burgers in town, on a lovely outside terrace.

3 Begijnhof > p.44. Tucked away off the Spui, this is an alluring, unusual oasis of peace in the heart of the city.

4 Amsterdam Museum > p.45. The history of the city, well told with lots of fascinating original artefacts and clever audiovisual touches, all housed in a former orphanage.

5 Red Light District > p.39. It's hard to come to Amsterdam and not have a wander around its most notorious neighbourhood.

6 Oude Kerk > p.38. Despite being right at the centre of the Red Light District, this is the city's most interesting and historic church.

7 Ons' Lieve Heer Op Solder > p.40. This clandestine Catholic church tucked away in an attic is a real delight.

Dinner at Van Kerkwijk > p.50. Great little bar/restaurant in the Old Centre. There's no menu – instead the friendly staff memorize the dishes of the day.

3

5

Jewish Amsterdam

Amsterdam's Jewish Quarter is a shadow of its former self, but there are many reminders of how integral to the life of the city its Jewish population once was. Touring these sights makes for a cohesive and moving day out, especially if you wind up at the most famous Jewish sight of them all, the Anne Frank Huis.

1 Waterlooplein > p.83. Home of the first Jewish settlement in Amsterdam, now the venue of the best flea market.

2 Joods Historisch Museum > p.85. Four converted synagogues house permanent and temporary exhibits on Jewish life in the city.

3 Esnoga > p.84. The city's Portuguese Synagogue was once one of the largest in the world.

2

4 Hollandse Schouwburg > p.87. The remains of a theatre that was the main assembly point for Jews being deported in World War II.

5 Wertheimpark > p.87. Tiny patch of greenery adorned by a moving memorial to those who died at Auschwitz.

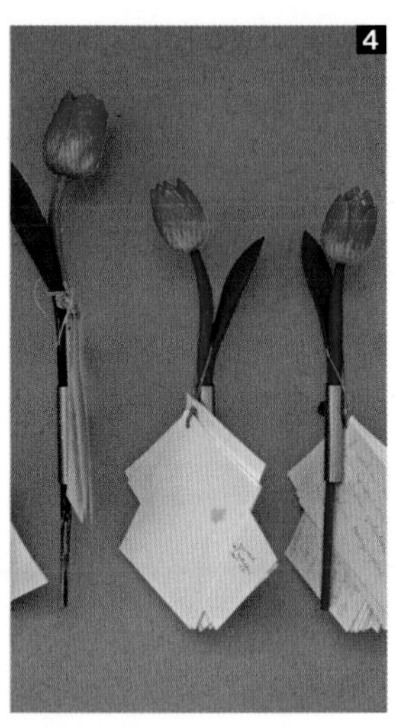
4

6 Verzetsmuseum > p.88. Excellent museum dedicated to the wartime resistance to the Germans.

Lunch at De Hortus > p.89. Coffee, cake and snacks inside the city's botanical gardens.

7 Gassan Diamonds > p.82. The only remnant of the main industry of the Jewish Quarter before the war.

8 Anne Frank Huis > p.57. Not in the Jewish Quarter proper, but still the city's principal – and only essential – Jewish sight.

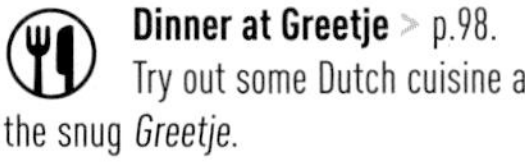

Dinner at Greetje > p.98. Try out some Dutch cuisine at the snug *Greetje*.

Free Amsterdam

It's possible to have a great day out in Amsterdam, see loads, and not spend a cent apart from a few euros on lunch and dinner. Here's how.

1 Schuttersgalerij > p.45. This gallery, with its portraits of civic guards, is the only free bit of the Amsterdam Museum.

2 Begijnhof > p.44. One of the city centre's most beguiling sights, and totally free.

3 Bloemenmarkt > p.63. There's no charge to wander past the stalls of the city's wonderful flower market.

Lunch from a street vendor > Join the locals and order a cone of *frites* and mayonnaise from one of the many street vendors.

4 Albert Cuypmarkt > p.109. Just wandering the length of the city's best market is a fine way to pass the time.

5 Lunchtime concerts at the Concertgebouw/Muziektheater > p.104/p.94. There are regular free lunchtime concerts at these two impressive music venues.

6 Vondelpark > p.105. The city centre's main park is one of its best attractions, and there's no charge for its weekend summer concerts either.

7 Zeeburg > p.94. Take a walk or, better, cycle around Amsterdam's up-and-coming districts to the east of Centraal Station.

8 Ferries across the IJ > p.96. Take one of the free ferries from behind Centraal Station to Amsterdam Noord and explore the emergent NDSM Shipyard or the EYE Film Institute.

Dinner at Bird > p.49. Fill up on Tom Yum soup, sweet spare ribs and well-priced vegetarian dishes at this busy little Thai canteen.

6

Amsterdam

BEST OF AMSTERDAM

Big sights

1 Van Gogh Museum With the world's most comprehensive collection of the artist's work, this museum is simply unmissable. > **p.103**

2 Red Light District Right or wrong, Amsterdam's red light district is the real thing – and a big attraction in its own right. > **p.39**

3 The Rijksmuseum The city's biggest and best art museum with a wonderful collection of Golden Age paintings. > **p.101**

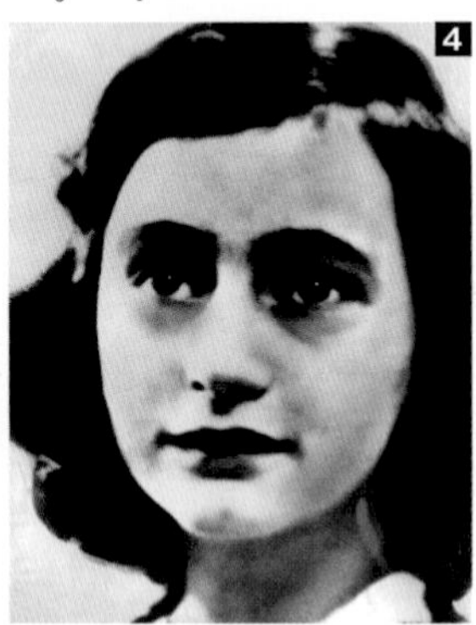

4 Anne Frank Huis The secret annexe where the diarist hid with her family during the German occupation is Amsterdam's most moving tourist attraction. > **p.57**

5 Koninklijk Paleis The supreme architectural example of the Dutch Golden Age, when the city was at the height of its powers. > **p.37**

Museums and galleries

1 Rijksmuseum The Rijksmuseum boasts an unrivalled collection of seventeenth-century Dutch art. > **p.101**

2 Ons' Lieve Heer op Solder Once a clandestine Catholic church, this seventeenth-century house chapel is an especially enjoyable sight. > **p.40**

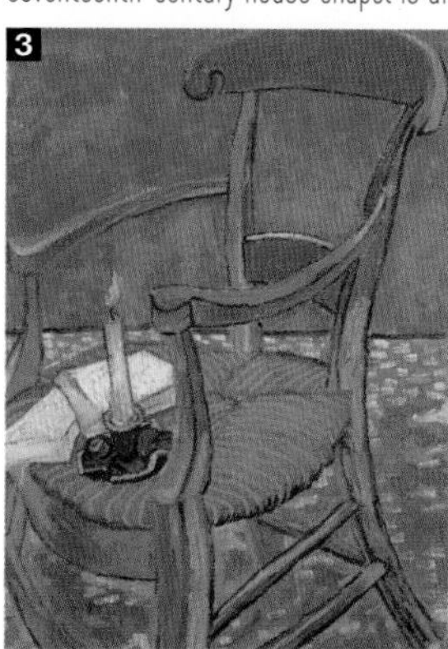

3 Van Gogh Museum The greatest collection of van Gogh's work, along with the contemporary paintings that influenced him. > **p.103**

4 Stedelijk Museum Amsterdam's world-class modern art museum is a prime attraction. > **p.104**

5 Amsterdam Museum An excellent museum devoted to the life and times of the city. > **p.45**

Waterfront

1 King's Day The one day of the year when anarchy reigns on the city's canals. Don't miss it. > **p.142**

2 Brouwersgracht The handsomely renovated former warehouses here make this one of the city's most picturesque canals. > **p.52**

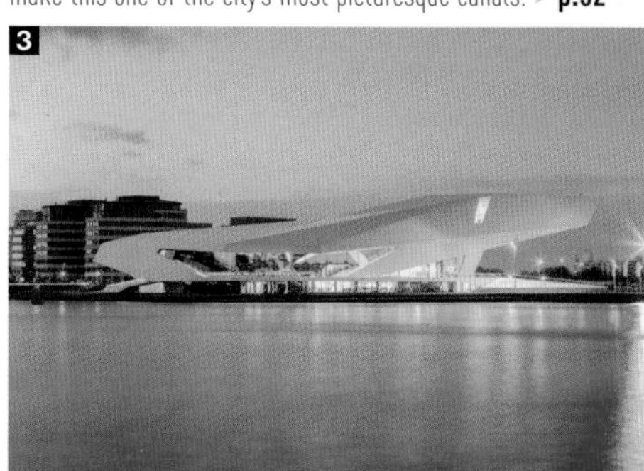

3 EYE The EYE Film Institute occupies the city's finest new building. > **p.96**

4 NDSM Shipyard Sprawling former shipyard now being renovated in style. > **p.96**

5 Zeeburg Cutting-edge new architecture and design, and lots of waterside bars and restaurants to enjoy it from. > **p.94**

Coffeeshops

1 Dampkring Loud and friendly city-centre hangout with excellent hash and weed at good prices. > **p.47**

2 Kadinsky Always busy, and serves great cookies and hot chocolate too. > **p.47**

3 Abraxas Lots of levels to negotiate via spiral staircases make this cosy place challenging after a spliff or two. > **p.47**

4 Barney's Once known for its great breakfast, now for the quality of its dope. > **p.76**

5 Hill Street Blues Favoured for its comfy sofas and chilled-out vibe, with a location right in the heart of the Red Light District. > **p.47**

Restaurants

1 Moeders Jordaan favourite where the quintessentially Dutch menu is overseen by photos of everyone's mother (*moeder*) > **p77**

2 Greetje Great service, fantastic modern Dutch food. > **p.98**

3 Blauw aan de Wal A wonderful, peaceful culinary haven right in the heart of the Red Light District. > **p.49**

4 Toscanini One of the city centre's best Italian restaurants – big, bustling and authentic. > **p.78**

5 De Belhamel Great-value Dutch cooking on picturesque Brouwersgracht. > **p.67**

Bars

1 Wynand Fockink Perhaps the city's best example of an old-fashioned *proeflokaal* or "tasting-house". > **p.51**

2 In 't Aepjen Right on Zeedijk, this is one of the city's top brown cafés. > **p.51**

2

4

4 Bubbles & Wines Around the corner from The Dam you'll find this polished bar with an outstanding range of wines and champagnes. > **p.50**

3

3 Arendsnest This friendly canal house bar is the best place to try Dutch beers from all over the country. > **p.69**

5 Het Papeneiland This rabbit warren of a place is one of the cosiest bars in the Grachtengordel. > **p.69**

5

Nights out

1 Melkweg The city's prime venue for inventive performing arts. > **p.70**

2 Jimmy Woo East meets West at this loungey club, where the stylish come out to play and the dancefloor heaves to the sound of disco and club classics. > **p.70**

3 Bitterzoet Spacious bar and theatre that hosts club nights and early evening live music and performance art. > **p.51**

4 Bimhuis Amsterdam's premier jazz and improvised music venue, sited right next door to the Muziekgebouw, beside the River IJ. > **p.99**

5 Paradiso One of the city's oldest venues for live music, and still one of the best. > **p.71**

Shopping

1 Puccini Bonboni The wonderful chocolates are made on the premises at Puccini's two city centre locations. > **p.47 & 65**

2 The Nine Streets De Negen Straatjes hosts some of the city's quirkiest one-off stores – well worth a wander. > **p.58**

3 Droog This design collective's Amsterdam HQ is quite unlike any other shop you may have been to and it's simply superb > **p.46**

4 Albert Cuypmarkt Busy general market that is still to some extent the authentic heart of working-class Amsterdam. > **p.109**

5 Jacob Hooij Traditional chemist famed for its Dutch liquorice. > **p.46**

PLACES

The Old Centre

Amsterdam's most vivacious district, the Old Centre is a tangle of antique streets and narrow canals, confined in the north by the River IJ and to the west and south by the Singel. Given the dominance of Centraal Station on most transport routes, this is where you'll almost certainly arrive. From here a stroll across the bridge will take you onto the Damrak, which divided the Oude Zijde (Old Side) of the medieval city to the east from the smaller Nieuwe Zijde (New Side) to the west. It also leads to the heart of the Old Centre, Dam Square – usually known as the Dam – the site of the city's most imperious building, the Royal Palace (Koninklijk Paleis). Nowadays much of the Oude Zijde is taken up by the city's notorious Red Light District – but the area is about more than just sleaze: its main canals and the houses that line them are among Amsterdam's most handsome. And the Old Centre as a whole hosts some of the city's best bars and restaurants alongside what can only be described as tourist tat.

CENTRAAL STATION

MAP PP.34–35, POCKET MAP C10–C11

At the time of its construction, on an artificial island in the 1880s, **Centraal Station** aroused much controversy because it effectively separated the centre from the River IJ, source of the city's wealth, for the first time in Amsterdam's long history. There was controversy about the choice of architect too: the man chosen, Petrus J.H. Cuypers, was Catholic, and in powerful Protestant circles there were mutterings about the vanity of his designs (he had recently completed the Rijksmuseum) and their unsuitability for Amsterdam. In the event, the station was built to Cuypers' design, but it was to be his last major commission; thereafter he spent most of his time building parish churches. Whatever you think about the building, it's certainly a good place to arrive. Its grand arches and cavernous main hall have a suitable sense of occasion, and from here all of the city lies before you.

TRAMS AT CENTRAAL STATION

ST NICOLAASKERK

ST NICOLAASKERK

Prins Hendrikkade 73 ⓣ 020 624 8749, ⓦ nicolaas-parochie.nl. Mon & Sat noon–3pm, Tues–Fri 11am–4pm. Free.
MAP PP.34–35, POCKET MAP D11

Dating back to the 1880s, the city's foremost Catholic church, with its whopping twin towers and spacious interior, is dedicated to the patron saint of sailors – and of Amsterdam. Above the altar is the crown of the Habsburg Emperor Maximilian, very much a symbol of the city.

DAMRAK

MAP PP.34–35, POCKET MAP C11

Running from Centraal Station to Dam Square, **Damrak** was a canal and the city's main nautical artery until 1672, when it was filled in – much to the relief of the locals, who were tired of the stink. With the docks moved elsewhere, Damrak became a busy commercial drag, as it remains today: a crowded avenue lined with tacky restaurants, bars and bureaux de change.

Toil and trouble: the Noord-Zuidlijn

Ask the average Amsterdammer about the **Noord-Zuidlijn** and they may start frothing at the mouth: the plan to build a super-fast, 10km-long metro line from the resurgent suburbs on the north side of the River IJ to a new transport hub on the south side of the city centre via Centraal Station may have seemed like a good idea when work began in 2003, but the execution has been little short of a disaster. For a start, **tunnelling** beneath the city centre proved far more difficult than the contractors had envisaged, not least because many of the city's older buildings rest on wooden stilts which are easily disturbed – as indeed the opponents of the scheme had predicted in the first place. Time and again work was delayed while buildings were shored up or reinforced, and as a consequence **costs** spiralled - the original estimate of €1.46 billion has risen to €3 billion and counting – and the **completion date** has been put back again and again (it's now 2017). Nevertheless, there are new municipal plans to extend the line to Schiphol airport – despite a collective groan from the opposition.

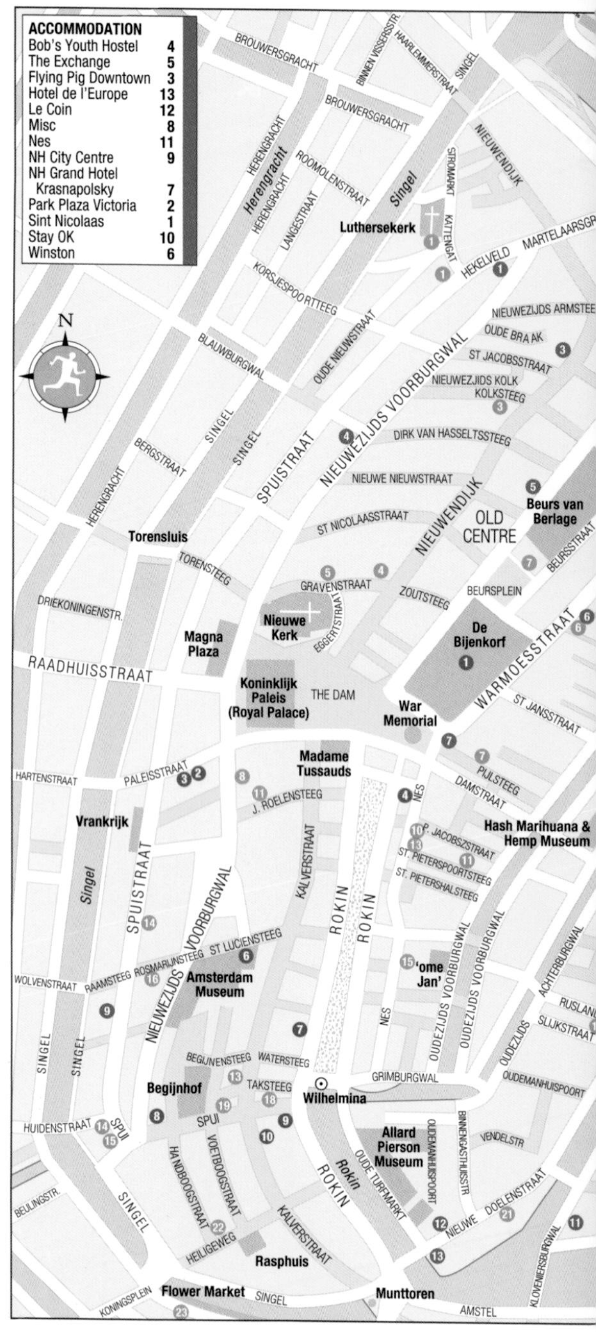
ACCOMMODATION
Bob's Youth Hostel 4
The Exchange 5
Flying Pig Downtown 3
Hotel de l'Europe 13
Le Coin 12
Misc 8
Nes 11
NH City Centre 9
NH Grand Hotel Krasnapolsky 7
Park Plaza Victoria 2
Sint Nicolaas 1
Stay OK 10
Winston 6
N
BROUWERSGRACHT
BINNEN VISSERSSTR.
HAARLEMMERSTRAAT
SINGEL
HERENGRACHT
Herengracht
ROOMOLENSTRAAT
LANGESTRAAT
Singel
STROMARKT
NIEUWENDIJK
KATTENGAT
Luthersekerk
HEKELVELD
MARTELAARSGR
KORSJESPOORTTEEG
NIEUWEZIJDS ARMSTEE
OUDE BRAAK
ST JACOBSSTRAAT
NIEUWEZIJDS KOLK
KOLKSTEEG
BLAUWBURGWAL
OUDE NIEUWSTRAAT
NIEUWEZIJDS VOORBURGWAL
DIRK VAN HASSELTSSTEEG
BERGSTRAAT
SPUISTRAAT
NIEUWE NIEUWSTRAAT
Beurs van Berlage
OLD CENTRE
ST NICOLAASSTRAAT
Torensluis
TORENSTEEG
BEURSSTRAAT
GRAVENSTRAAT
ZOUTSTEEG
BEURSPLEIN
DRIEKONINGENSTR.
Nieuwe Kerk
EGGERTSTRAAT
De Bijenkorf
Magna Plaza
WARMOESSTRAAT
RAADHUISSTRAAT
Koninklijk Paleis (Royal Palace)
THE DAM
War Memorial
ST JANSSTRAAT
Madame Tussauds
HARTENSTRAAT
PALEISSTRAAT
J. ROELENSTEEG
NES
PIJLSTEEG
DAMSTRAAT
Vrankrijk
P. JACOBSZSTRAAT
ST. PIETERSPOORTSTEEG
ST. PIETERSHALSTEEG
Hash Marihuana & Hemp Museum
KALVERSTRAAT
ROKIN
ROSMARIJNSTEEG
ST LUCIENSTEEG
'ome Jan'
OUDEZIJDS VOORBURGWAL
ACHTERBURGWAL
WOLVENSTRAAT
RAAMSTEEG
Amsterdam Museum
RUSLAND
SLIJKSTRAAT
BEGIJNENSTEEG
WATERSTEEG
GRIMBURGWAL
OUDEMANHUISPOORT
Begijnhof
TAKSTEEG
Wilhelmina
HUIDENSTRAAT
SPUI
VOETBOOGSTRAAT
HANDBOOGSTRAAT
Allard Pierson Museum
BINNENGASTHUISSTR.
VENDELSTR
OUDE TURFMARKT
Rokin
DOELENSTRAAT
NIEUWE
BEULINGSTR.
HEILIGEWEG
Rasphuis
KLOVENIERSBURGWAL
KONINGSPLEIN
Flower Market
Munttoren
AMSTEL

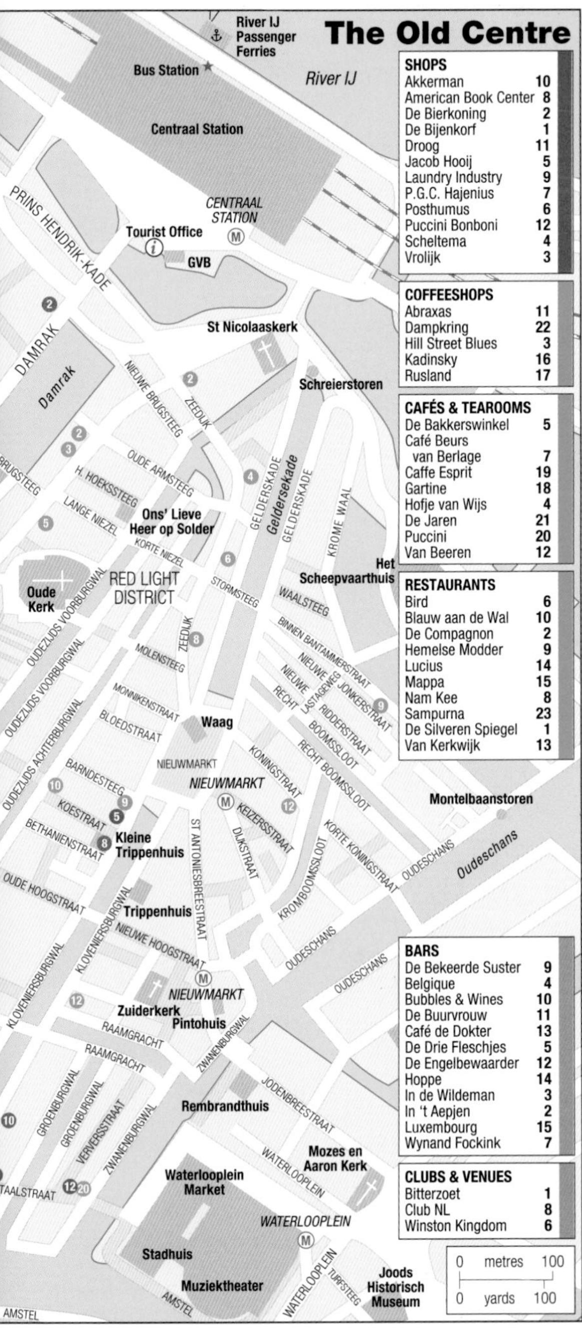
The Old Centre
SHOPS
Akkerman 10
American Book Center 8
De Bierkoning 2
De Bijenkorf 1
Droog 11
Jacob Hooij 5
Laundry Industry 9
P.G.C. Hajenius 7
Posthumus 6
Puccini Bonboni 12
Scheltema 4
Vrolijk 3
COFFEESHOPS
Abraxas 11
Dampkring 22
Hill Street Blues 3
Kadinsky 16
Rusland 17
CAFÉS & TEAROOMS
De Bakkerswinkel 5
Café Beurs van Berlage 7
Caffe Esprit 19
Gartine 18
Hofje van Wijs 4
De Jaren 21
Puccini 20
Van Beeren 12
RESTAURANTS
Bird 6
Blauw aan de Wal 10
De Compagnon 2
Hemelse Modder 9
Lucius 14
Mappa 15
Nam Kee 8
Sampurna 23
De Silveren Spiegel 1
Van Kerkwijk 13
BARS
De Bekeerde Suster 9
Belgique 4
Bubbles & Wines 10
De Buurvrouw 11
Café de Dokter 13
De Drie Fleschjes 5
De Engelbewaarder 12
Hoppe 14
In de Wildeman 3
In 't Aepjen 2
Luxembourg 15
Wynand Fockink 7
CLUBS & VENUES
Bitterzoet 1
Club NL 8
Winston Kingdom 6
0 metres 100
0 yards 100
River IJ Passenger Ferries
River IJ
Bus Station
Centraal Station
CENTRAAL STATION
Tourist Office
GVB
PRINS HENDRIK-KADE
St Nicolaaskerk
DAMRAK
Damrak
Schreierstoren
NIEUWE BRUGSTEEG
ZEEDIJK
OUDE ARMSTEEG
H. HOEKSSTEEG
LANGE NIEZEL
BRUGSTEEG
Ons' Lieve Heer op Solder
KORTE NIEZEL
GELDERSKADE
Geldersekade
KROME WAAL
Het Scheepvaarthuis
Oude Kerk
RED LIGHT DISTRICT
OUDEZIJDS VOORBURGWAL
STORMSTEEG
WAALSTEEG
BINNEN BANTAMMERSTRAAT
NIEUWE JONKERSTRAAT
NIEUWE LASTAGEWEG
RECHT RIDDERSTRAAT
BOOMSSLOOT
RECHT BOOMSSLOOT
MOLENSTEEG
MONNIKENSTRAAT
BLOEDSTRAAT
Waag
OUDEZIJDS ACHTERBURGWAL
NIEUWMARKT
KONINGSTRAAT
Montelbaanstoren
BARNDESTEEG
KOESTRAAT
BETHANIENSTRAAT
Kleine Trippenhuis
ST ANTONIESBREESTRAAT
KEIZERSSTRAAT
DIJKSTRAAT
KORTE KONINGSTRAAT
KROMBOOMSSLOOT
OUDESCHANS
Oudeschans
OUDE HOOGSTRAAT
Trippenhuis
KLOVENIERSBURGWAL
NIEUWE HOOGSTRAAT
Zuiderkerk
Pintohuis
RAAMGRACHT
ZWANENBURGWAL
JODENBREESTRAAT
GROENBURGWAL
VERVERSSTRAAT
Rembrandthuis
Mozes en Aaron Kerk
WATERLOOPLEIN
Waterlooplein Market
STAALSTRAAT
Stadhuis
Muziektheater
AMSTEL
TURFSTEEG
Joods Historisch Museum

CYCLING IN DOWNTOWN AMSTERDAM

BEURS VAN BERLAGE

Damrak 243 ⓣ 020 530 4141, ⓦ beursvanberlage.com. Mon–Fri 10am–10pm, Fri & Sat 9.30am–10pm. €24.50. MAP PP.34–35, POCKET MAP B11–C11

The imposing bulk of the **Beurs** – the old Stock Exchange – is a seminal work designed at the turn of the twentieth century by the leading light of the Dutch modern movement, **Hendrik Petrus Berlage**. Berlage re-routed Dutch architecture with this building, forsaking the classicism that had dominated the nineteenth century for a modern style with cleaner lines. The Beurs has long since lost its commercial function and today it's used for exhibitions, concerts and conferences, which means that sometimes you can go in, sometimes you can't. Inside, the main hall is distinguished by the graceful lines of its exposed ironwork and its shallow-arched arcades as well as the fanciful frieze celebrating the stockbroker's trade. If it's closed, stop by the café that fronts onto Beursplein around the corner (see p.48) for a coffee and admire the tiled scenes of the past, present and the future by Jan Toorop.

THE DAM

MAP PP.34–35, POCKET MAP B12

At the very heart of the city, **Dam Square** –usually known as **The Dam** – gave Amsterdam its name: in the thirteenth century the River Amstel was dammed here, and the fishing village that grew around it became known as "Amstelredam". Boats could sail into the Dam down the Damrak and unload right in the middle of the settlement, which soon prospered by trading herrings for Baltic grain. Today it's an open and airy but somehow rather desultory square, despite the presence of the main municipal war memorial, a prominent stone tusk adorned by bleak, suffering figures and decorated with the coats of arms of each of the Netherlands' provinces (plus the ex-colony of Indonesia).

MADAME TUSSAUDS

Dam 20 ⓣ 020 522 1010, ⓦ www.madametussauds.com/amsterdam. Daily 10am–6.30pm. €23.50, children 5–15 €19.50. MAP PP.34–35, POCKET MAP B12

The Amsterdam branch of the **Madame Tussauds** empire provides waxwork Dutch royals and footballers alongside the usual international celebs.

KONINKLIJK PALEIS

The Dam ⓣ 020 522 6161, ⓦ paleisamsterdam.nl. Daily: April–Sept 10am–5pm; Oct–March 11am–5pm, but closed on Royal occasions as detailed on the website. €10. MAP PP.34–35, POCKET MAP B12

Dominating The Dam is the **Koninklijk Paleis** (Royal Palace) though the title is deceptive, given that this vast structure started out as the city's town hall and only had its first royal occupant when Louis Bonaparte, brother of Napoleon, moved in during the French occupation.

At the time of the building's construction in the mid-seventeenth century, Amsterdam was at the height of its powers, and the city council craved a residence that was a suitable declaration of its wealth and independence. The **exterior** is full of maritime symbolism, hinting at the trade routes that made the city rich. The **interior** proclaims the pride and confidence of Amsterdam's Golden Age, principally in the lavish **Citizen's Hall** where the enthroned figure of Amsterdam looks down on the earth and the heavens, laid out before her in three circular, inlaid marble maps. Other allegorical **figures** ram home the municipal point: flanking "Amsterdam" to the left and right are Wisdom and Strength, and the relief to the right shows Mercury attempting to lull Argos to sleep – stressing the need to be vigilant. All this is part of a witty symbolism that pervades the Hall and the surrounding galleries: in the top-left gallery, cocks fight above the entrance to the Commissioner of Petty Affairs and above the door of the Bankruptcy Chamber, in the gallery to the right of the main hall, a medallion shows the Fall of Icarus below marble carvings depicting hungry rats nibbling at unpaid bills.

The decorative whimsy fizzles out in the intimidating and cramped **High Court of Justice** at the front of the building. Here, magistrates sat on marble benches overseen by heavyweight representations of Righteousness, Wisdom and Mercy as they passed judgement on the hapless criminals in front of them; even worse, the baying crowd on The Dam could view the proceedings through the barred windows. If a death sentence was passed, the condemned was whisked up to a wooden scaffold attached to the front of the building and promptly dispatched.

THE KONINKLIJK PALEIS

OUDE KERK

NIEUWE KERK

The Dam ⓣ 020 638 6909, ⓦ nieuwekerk.nl. Hours vary with exhibitions, but core hours daily 11am–5pm. Admission varies; from €8. MAP PP.34–35, POCKET MAP B12

Vying for importance with the Royal Palace is the adjacent **Nieuwe Kerk**, which despite its name – "new church" – is an early fifteenth-century structure built in a late flourish of the Gothic style, with a forest of pinnacles and high, slender gables. Nowadays it's de-sanctified and used for temporary exhibitions. Opening times vary, and occasionally it's closed altogether when exhibitions are being changed, but it is worth going in if you can: its hangar-like interior holds a scattering of decorative highlights, such as the seventeenth-century tomb of Dutch naval hero Admiral Michiel de Ruyter, complete with trumpeting angels, conch-blowing Neptunes and cherubs all in a tizzy.

MAGNA PLAZA

Nieuwezijds Voorburgwal 182 ⓦ magnaplaza.nl. Mon 11am–7pm, Tues–Sat 10am–7pm, Thurs until 9pm, Sun noon–7pm. MAP PP.34–35, POCKET MAP A12

Behind the Royal Palace, you can't miss the old neo-Gothic post office of 1899, now converted into the **Magna Plaza** shopping mall, housing numerous clothes chains.

OUDE KERK

Oudekerksplein ⓣ 020 625 8284, ⓦ oudekerk.nl. Church: Mon–Sat 10am–6pm, Sun 1–5.30pm; €7.50. MAP PP.34–35, POCKET MAP C12

Tucked away in the Red Light District, the **Oude Kerk** is the city's most appealing church. There's been a church on this site since the middle of the thirteenth century, but most of the present building dates from a century later, funded by the pilgrims who came here in their hundreds following a widely publicized miracle. The story goes that in 1345 a dying man regurgitated the Host he had received here at Communion and when it was thrown on the fire afterwards, it did not burn. The unburnable Host was placed in a chest and eventually installed here, and although it disappeared during the Reformation, thousands of the faithful still come to take part in the annual commemorative **Stille Omgang** in mid-March, a silent nocturnal procession terminating at the Oude Kerk.

Inside the church you can see the unadorned memorial tablet of Rembrandt's first wife, Saskia van Uylenburg, beneath (and just to the left of) the smaller of the organs, and four beautifully coloured stained-glass windows beside the ambulatory dating from the 1550s.

The Red Light District

The area to the east of Damrak, between Warmoesstraat, Nieuwmarkt and Damstraat, is the **Red Light District**, known locally as "De Walletjes" (Small Walls) on account of the series of low brick walls that contains its canals. The district stretches across the two narrow canals that once marked the eastern limits of medieval Amsterdam, **Oudezijds Voorburgwal** and **Oudezijds Achterburgwal**. The area is pretty seedy, although the legalized prostitution here has long been one of the city's most distinctive draws. It wasn't always so: the handsome facades of Oudezijds Voorburgwal in particular recall ritzier days when this was one of the wealthiest parts of the city, richly earning its nickname the "Velvet Canal".

Oudezijds Voorburgwal and Oudezijds Achterburgwal, with their narrow connecting passages, are thronged with "**window brothels**", and at busy times the crass, on-street haggling over the price of sex is drowned out by a surprisingly festive atmosphere – entire families grinning more or less amiably at the women in the windows or discussing the specifications of the sex toys in the shops. Nonetheless, there is an unpleasant undertow to the district, oddly enough sharper during the daytime, despite the best efforts of the police, who keep the pimps and the junkies pretty much at bay. Don't even think about taking a picture of one of the window brothels, unless you're prepared for some major grief from the camera-shy prostitutes and their minders.

What's more, the whole **future** of the Red Light District is under threat. The trafficking of women to fill the window brothels – and the concomitant illegal clandestine brothels – has become something of a municipal scandal and there have been political manoeuvres to have the whole area closed down or moved way out of the city. At the moment, there's a deadlock in the situation, but it's hard to say quite how the issue will be resolved.

ONS' LIEVE HEER OP SOLDER

Oudezijds Voorburgwal 38 ⓣ 020 624 6604, ⓦ opsolder.nl. Mon–Sat 10am–5pm, Sun 1–5pm. €10. MAP PP.34–35, POCKET MAP C11

A few metres north of the Oude Kerk (see p.38) is the lovely **Ons' Lieve Heer op Solder** ("our Dear Lord in the Attic"), a former Catholic chapel, now one of Amsterdam's most enjoyable museums. The church dates from the early seventeenth century when the city's ruling Protestants decreed that Catholics could no longer practise their faith openly. The result was an eccentric compromise: Catholics were allowed to hold services in any private building providing that the exterior revealed no sign of their activities – hence the development of the city's **clandestine churches** (*schuilkerken*), of which the Ons' Lieve Heer op Solder is the only one to have survived intact, here in the loft of a wealthy merchant's house. The church's narrow nave has been skilfully shoehorned into the available space and, flanked by elegant balconies, there's just enough room for an ornately carved organ at one end and a mock-marble high altar, decorated with Jacob de Wit's mawkish *Baptism of Christ*, at the other. The rest of the house is similarly untouched, its original furnishings reminiscent of interiors by Vermeer or De Hooch.

ONS' LIEVE HEER OP SOLDER

HASH MARIHUANA & HEMP MUSEUM

Oudezijds Achterburgwal 148 ⓣ 020 624 8926, ⓦ hashmuseum.com. Daily 10am–10pm. €9. MAP PP.34–35, POCKET MAP C12

The **Hash Marihuana & Hemp Museum** claims to hold the "world's largest collection of cannabis-related artefacts" and features displays on different kinds of dope and the huge number of ways to imbibe and otherwise use it. Among the six thousand items on show are old tins of prescription cannabis, a hemp electric guitar and running shoes, plus pamphlets explaining the medicinal properties of weed. There's also a shop selling pipes, books, videos and plenty of souvenirs.

NIEUWMARKT

MAP PP.34–35, POCKET MAP C12

On the far side of the Red Light District is the Nieuwmarkt, a wide open cobbled square that was long one of the city's most important markets. Its focus is the multi-turreted **Waag**, a delightful building dating from the 1480s, when it served as one of the city's fortified gates, the Sint Antoniespoort. Thereafter it was turned into a municipal weighing-house (*waag*), with the rooms upstairs taken over by the surgeons' guild. It was here that the surgeons held lectures on anatomy and public dissections, the inspiration for

Rembrandt's famous *Anatomy Lesson of Dr Tulp*. It has now been converted into a café-bar and restaurant, *In de Waag*.

SCHREIERSTOREN

Geldersekade. MAP PP.34–35, POCKET MAP D11–D12

A few minutes' walk north from Nieuwmarkt, the squat **Schreierstoren** (Weepers' Tower) is a rare surviving chunk of the city's medieval wall. Originally, the tower overlooked the River IJ and it was here (legend has it) that women gathered to watch their menfolk sail away – hence its name. A badly weathered stone plaque inserted in the wall is a reminder of all those sad goodbyes, and another much more recent plaque recalls the departure of Henry Hudson from here in 1609, when he stumbled across an island the locals called Manhattan.

HET SCHEEPVAARTHUIS

Prins Hendrikkade 108 MAP PP.34–35, POCKET MAP D12

Now occupied by the five-star *Amrath* hotel, this is one of the city's most flamboyant Expressionist buildings, covered with a welter of maritime references – the entrance is shaped like the prow of a ship, and surmounted by statues of Poseidon and his wife, and representations of the four points of the compass.

KLOVENIERSBURGWAL

MAP PP.34–35, POCKET MAP C12–C13

Nieuwmarkt lies at the northern end of **Kloveniersburgwal**, a long, dead-straight waterway framed by old, dignified facades. One house of special note is the **Trippenhuis**, at no. 29, a huge overblown mansion built for the Trip family in 1662. One of the richest families in Amsterdam, the Trips were one of a clique of families (Six, Trip, Hooft and Pauw) who shared power during the city's Golden Age.

Almost directly opposite the Trippenhuis, on the west bank of the canal, the **Kleine Trippenhuis** at no. 26 is, by contrast, one of the narrowest houses in Amsterdam, complete with a warmly carved facade with a balustrade featuring centaurs and sphinxes. Legend asserts that Mr Trip's coachman was so taken aback by the size of the new family mansion that he exclaimed he would be happy with a home no wider than the Trips' front door – which is exactly what he got.

ST ANTONIESBREESTRAAT

MAP PP.34–35, POCKET MAP C12–C13

Stretching south from the wide open spaces of the Nieuwmarkt, **St Antoniesbreestraat** once linked the city centre with the Jewish quarter, but its huddle of shops and houses was mostly demolished in the 1980s to make way for a main road. The plan was subsequently abandoned, but the modern buildings that now line most of the street hardly fire the soul, even if the modern symmetries – and cubist, coloured panels – of the apartment blocks do lighten the aesthetic gloom.

PINTOHUIS

St Antoniesbreestraat 69 ⓣ 020 370 0210, ⓦ huisdepinto.nl. Mon–Fri 10.30am–5.30pm, Sat 1–5pm. Free. MAP PP.34–35, POCKET MAP D13

One of the few survivors of all the development along St Antoniebreestraat is the **Pintohuis**, which is now a public library. Easily spotted by its creamy Italianate facade, the mansion is named after Isaac de Pinto, a Jew who fled Portugal to escape the Inquisition and subsequently became a founder of the East India Company. Pinto bought the property in 1651 and promptly had it remodelled in grand style, the facade interrupted by six lofty pilasters, which lead the eye up to the blind balustrade. The mansion was the talk of the town, even more so when Pinto had the interior painted in a similar style to the front – pop in to look at the birds and cherubs of the original painted ceiling.

PINTOHUIS

ZUIDERKERK

Zuiderkerkhof ⓣ 020 308 0399, ⓦ zuiderkerkamsterdam.nl. Open for special events and concerts only. MAP PP.34–35, POCKET MAP C13

The **Zuiderkerk** dates from 1611 and was designed by the prolific architect and sculptor Hendrick de Keyser, whose distinctive – and very popular – style extrapolated elements of traditional Flemish design, with fanciful detail added wherever possible. The soaring tower is typical of his work and comes complete with balconies and balustrades, arches and columns. The church was deconsecrated in the 1930s, and it was here that the bodies of the dead were temporarily stored and piled up during the terrible winter – the "Hunger Winter" – of 1944–45.

OUDEMANHUISPOORT

MAP PP.34–35, POCKET MAP B14

At the south end of Kloveniersburgwal, on the right, the **Oudemanhuispoort** is a covered passageway whose sides are lined with secondhand bookstalls (Mon–Thurs 8am–10pm, Fri 8am–5pm); it was formerly part of an almshouse complex for elderly men – hence the unusual name. The buildings to either side of

ZUIDERKERK

the passageway are now part of the University of Amsterdam, which dominates this part of town, its associated colleges and residences stretching south to Nieuwe Dolenstraat.

STAALSTRAAT

MAP PP.34–35, POCKET MAP C14

A dinky little bridge spans the southern end of Kloveniersburgwal to reach pedestrianized **Staalstraat**, which cuts across one of the most picturesque corners of the city on its way to Waterlooplein (see p.83). Staalstraat offers an especially lovely view down Groenburgwal, a narrow and almost impossibly pretty waterway framed by dignified old canal houses with the Zuiderkerk looming beyond.

ROKIN AND KALVERSTRAAT

MAP PP.34–35, POCKET MAP B12–B14

The **Rokin** picks up where the Damrak leaves off, cutting south from the Dam in a wide sweep that follows the former course of the River Amstel. This was the business centre of the nineteenth-century city, and although it has lost much of its prestige, it is still flanked by an attractive medley of architectural styles incorporating everything from grandiose nineteenth-century mansions to more utilitarian modern stuff. Running parallel, pedestrianized **Kalverstraat** is a busy shopping street that has been a commercial centre since medieval times, when it was used as a calf market; nowadays it's mostly chain stores and clothes shops – you could be anywhere in Europe really.

ALLARD PIERSON MUSEUM

Oude Turfmarkt 127 ⓣ 020 525 2556, ⓦ allardpiersonmuseum.nl. Tues–Sun 10am–5pm, also Mon in school hols. €10. MAP PP.34–35, POCKET MAP B13–B14

The **Allard Pierson Museum** is a good old-fashioned archeological museum spread over two floors. It's not an especially large collection, but it does have a wide-ranging assortment of artefacts mainly retrieved from Egypt, Greece and Italy. The ground floor is used for temporary exhibitions and the Egyptian pieces, among which is a fascinating section on the **Coptic Christians**, who still account for around ten percent (eight million) of the Egyptian population. Also of note is a delightful model of a ship and its crew from the Middle Kingdom: a funerary object designed to transport the soul of the dead to the afterlife. Upstairs, the highlight is the museum's Greek **pottery**, with superb examples of both the black- and red-figured wares produced in the sixth and fifth centuries BC. Look out also for several ornate Roman **sarcophagi** – especially the whopper made of marble and decorated with Dionysian scenes – as well as Etruscan funerary urns and carvings.

HEILIGEWEG AND SPUI

MAP PP.34-35, POCKET MAP A14

Heiligeweg, or "Holy Way", which crosses Kalverstraat near Muntplein, was once part of a much longer route used by pilgrims heading into Amsterdam. All religious references disappeared centuries ago, but there is one interesting edifice here, the fanciful gateway of the old **Rasphuis** (House of Correction) that now fronts a shopping mall at the foot of Voetboogstraat. The gateway is surmounted by a sculpture of a woman punishing two criminals chained at her sides above the single word "Castigatio" (punishment). Beneath is a carving by Hendrik de Keyser showing wolves and lions cringing before the whip.

Cut up Voetboogstraat and you soon reach the **Spui**, which opens out into a wide, tram-clanking intersection. Right in the middle is a cloying statue of a young boy, known as *'t Lieverdje* ("Little Darling" or "Loveable Scamp"), a gift to the city from a cigarette company in 1960. It was here in the mid-1960s, with the statue seen as a symbol of the addicted consumer, that those playful political mavericks and situationists, the anarchic **Provos**, organized some of their most successful public pranks. There's a small secondhand book market here on Friday mornings.

BEGIJNHOF

Spui ⓣ 020 622 1918, ⓦ begijnhofamsterdam.nl. Daily 9am–5pm. Free. MAP PP.34-35, POCKET MAP A13

A little gateway on the north side of the Spui leads into the **Begijnhof**, where a huddle of immaculately maintained old houses looks onto a central green; if this door is locked, try the main entrance, 200m north of the Spui on Gedempte Begijnensloot. The Begijnhof was founded in the fourteenth century as a home for the *beguines* – members of a Catholic sisterhood living as nuns, but without vows and with the right of return to the secular world. The original medieval complex comprised a series of humble brick cottages, but these were mostly replaced by the larger, grander houses of today shortly after the Reformation, though the secretive, enclosed design survived.

The **Engelse Kerk**, beside the

THE BEGIJNHOF

central green, is of medieval construction, but it was taken from the *beguines* and given to Amsterdam's English community during the Reformation. It's of interest for the carefully worked panels on the pulpit, which were designed by a youthful Piet Mondriaan. The *beguines*, meanwhile, celebrated Mass inconspicuously in the clandestine Catholic **Begijnhof Kapel**, which they established in the house opposite their old church, and this is still used today, a homely and very devout place, full of paintings and with large balconies on either side of the main nave.

AMSTERDAM MUSEUM

Sint Luciënsteeg 27 & Kalverstraat 92 020 523 1822, amsterdammuseum.nl. Daily 10am–5pm. €12.50; audio-tour €4. MAP PP.34–35, POCKET MAP A13

The **Amsterdam Museum**, which occupies the rambling seventeenth-century buildings of the former municipal orphanage, surveys the city's development from its origins as an insignificant fishing village to its present incarnation as a major metropolis. A visit begins with an overview by means of a series of short films branded as "**Amsterdam DNA**"; film clips run continuously giving an insight into key events that have shaped the city's history.

Thereafter, the museum spreads over three main floors, and gets rather more confusing as you negotiate its many levels and corridors – be sure to collect a museum map at the ticket office. Broadly, the ground floor concentrates on the Golden Age; the first floor focuses on the eighteenth and nineteenth centuries; and the second floor deals with the modern era, from 1940 onwards. The latter is perhaps the most intriguing section, covering a wide range of topics, notably the German occupation of World War II; the demise of the Amsterdam shipbuilding industry; the squatters' movement; and the Provos (see opposite). Here also is a so-called "White Car" – *De Witkar* – which looks something like a golf buggy and was part of an early environmental move to do something about the city's traffic congestion: the idea was that these simple, publically owned vehicles would be the only ones allowed in the city centre. By 1979, there were 35 on the road, but the more reactionary climate of the 1980s put paid to the whole idea.

AMSTERDAM MUSEUM

Attached to the main body of the museum is an open-air **courtyard**, where a set of wooden lockers show where the orphans would stow their kit, and a **glassed-in passageway** – the schuttersgalerij – which is used for temporary exhibitions of group portraits – anything from Johan Cruyff and his footballing chums to paintings of the Amsterdam militia in their seventeenth-century pomp.

Shops

AKKERMAN

Langebrugsteeg 13 T 020 623 1649, W pwakkerman.nl. Mon–Fri 9am–5.30pm, Sat 10am–5pm & Sun 1–5pm. MAP PP.34–35, POCKET MAP B13

This is far and away the city's poshest pen shop, with an excellent selection of pens and writing accessories.

AMERICAN BOOK CENTER

Spui 12 T 020 635 5537, W abc.nl. Mon noon–8pm, Tues–Sat 10am–8pm & Sun 11am–6.30pm. MAP PP.34–35, POCKET MAP A13

This place has a great stock of books in English, and is one of the city's best sources of English-language magazines and newspapers.

DE BIERKONING

Paleisstraat 125 T 020 625 2336, W bierkoning.nl. Mon–Sat 11am–7pm & Sun 1–6pm. MAP PP.34–35, POCKET MAP A12

The "Beer King" is aptly named: 950 different beers, with the appropriate glasses to drink them from – just in case you thought beer-drinking could be taken lightly.

DROOG

DE BIJENKORF

Dam 1 W debijenkorf.nl. Sun & Mon 11am–8pm, Tues & Wed 10am–8pm, Thurs & Fri 10am–9pm, Sat 9.30am–8pm. MAP PP.34–35, POCKET MAP B12

The city's top department store, good for clothes, accessories and kids' stuff.

DROOG

Staalstraat 7b W droog.com. Tues & Wed 11am–6pm, Thurs–Sun 11am–7pm. MAP PP.34–35, POCKET MAP C14

The Amsterdam HQ of the Dutch design collective is a shrine to both simplicity and artsiness, with attention-grabbing furniture, clothes and household objects.

JACOB HOOIJ

Kloveniersburgwal 12 T 020 624 3041, W www.jacob-hooy.nl. Mon 1–6pm, Tues–Fri 10am–6pm, Sat 10am–5pm. MAP PP.34–35, POCKET MAP C12

In business at this address since 1778, this is a traditional homeopathic chemist with any amount of herbs and natural cosmetics, as well as a huge stock of *drop* (Dutch liquorice).

LAUNDRY INDUSTRY

Spui 1 T 020 420 2554, W laundryindustry.com. Tues–Sat 11am–6pm & Sun noon–6pm. MAP PP.34–35, POCKET MAP B13

Main Amsterdam branch of this cool high-end Dutch womenswear brand: great clothes, and a nice environment for browsing.

P.G.C. HAJENIUS

Rokin 92 T 020 623 7494, W hajenius.com. Mon noon–6pm, Tues–Sat 9.30am–6pm, Sun noon–5pm. MAP PP.34–35, POCKET MAP B13

Long-established tobacconist selling its own and other brands of cigars, tobacco, smoking accessories, and just about every make of cigarette you can think of.

POSTHUMUS

Sint Luciensteeg 23 ⓣ 020 625 5812, ⓦ posthumuswinkel.nl. Tues–Fri 9am–5pm, Sat 11am–5pm. MAP PP.34–35, POCKET MAP A13
Top-of-the-range stationery, cards and, best of all, a choice of hundreds of rubber stamps.

PUCCINI BONBONI

Staalstraat 17 ⓣ 020 626 5474, ⓦ puccini.nl. Sun & Mon noon–6pm, Tues–Sat 11am–6pm. MAP PP.34–35, POCKET MAP C14
Probably the best chocolate shop in town – all handmade, with an array of fantastic and imaginative fillings.

SCHELTEMA

Rokin 9–15 ⓣ 020 523 1411, ⓦ scheltema.nl. Mon 11am–8pm, Tues, Sat & Sun 10am–8pm, Wed–Fri 10am–9pm. MAP PP.34–35, POCKET MAP B12
Amsterdam's biggest and best bookshop is over several floors. Although most of the books are in Dutch, there are good English sections too.

VROLIJK

Paleisstraat 135 ⓣ 020 623 5142, ⓦ vrolijk.nu. Mon–Sat 11am–6pm & Sun noon–6pm. MAP PP.34–35, POCKET MAP A12
This is the largest LGBT bookshop in Europe, with books, magazines and dvds.

ABRAXAS

Coffeeshops

ABRAXAS

Jonge Roelensteeg 12 ⓣ 020 625 5763. Daily 10am–1am. MAP PP.34–35, POCKET MAP B12
Quirky coffeeshop with spiral staircases that are challenging after a spliff. The hot chocolate with hash is not for the susceptible.

DAMPKRING

Handboogstraat 29 Daily 10am–1am. MAP PP.34–35, POCKET MAP A14
Colourful coffeeshop with a laidback atmosphere that is known for its range of good-quality weed and hash. Used as a location in *Ocean's Twelve* starring Brad Pitt.

HILL STREET BLUES

Warmeosstraat 52a ⓣ 020 638 7922. Daily 9am–1am, Fri & Sat until 3am. MAP PP.34–35, POCKET MAP C11
Grungy, heavily graffitied coffeeshop full of comfy chairs with a good vibe and a drum'n'bass soundtrack. In the Red Light District.

KADINSKY

Rosmarijnsteeg 9 ⓣ 020 420 4686. Daily 9.30am–1am. MAP PP.34–35, POCKET MAP A13
The pick of a small chain; cozy and intimate with good deals, excellent chocolate chip cookies and a jazzy soundtrack.

RUSLAND

Rusland 16 ⓣ 020 845 6434. Daily 10am–1am. MAP PP.34–35, POCKET MAP C13
One of the first Amsterdam coffeeshops, a cramped but vibrant place that's a favourite with both dope fans and tea addicts (it has forty different kinds).

Cafés and tearooms

DE BAKKERSWINKEL

Warmoesstraat 69 ⓣ 020 489 8000, ⓦ bakkerswinkel.nl. Mon–Fri 8am–5.30pm, Sat & Sun 9am–6pm. MAP PP.34–35, POCKET MAP C11

One of a popular chain offering delicious home-made scones with lemon curd and jam, muffins, cakes, quiches and pies for €5–10. Don't be surprised if you have to queue at lunchtime.

CAFÉ BEURS VAN BERLAGE

Beursplein 1 ⓣ 020 530 4146, ⓦ beursvanberlage.nl. Mon–Sat 10am–6pm, Sun 11am–6pm. MAP PP.34–35, POCKET MAP B12

The best chance to glimpse the interior of the Beurs, and an attractively furnished place to drink coffee or eat lunch.

CAFFE ESPRIT

Spui 10 ⓣ 020 616 8660, ⓦ caffeesprit.nl. Mon–Wed & Sun 10am–6pm, Thurs 10am–8pm, Fri & Sat 10am–7pm. MAP PP.34–35, POCKET MAP A13

This ultra-modern café, overlooking the Spui, has a whopping terrace and serves generously filled sandwiches and superb salads, as well as more substantial meals.

HOFJE VAN WIJS

GARTINE

Taksteeg 7 ⓣ 020 320 4132, ⓦ gartine.nl. Wed–Sun 10am–6pm. MAP PP.34–35, POCKET MAP B13

Tiny place off one of the grungier stretches of Kalverstraat. Nice breakfasts, an array of inventive sandwiches for lunch, and then – their speciality – high tea served in the afternoon.

HOFJE VAN WIJS

Zeedijk 43 ⓣ 020 624 0436, ⓦ hofjevanwijs.nl. Tues–Sat noon–4pm & 6–10.30pm, Sun noon–4pm & 6–9pm. MAP PP.34–35, POCKET MAP D11

A hidden treasure in an eighteenth-century courtyard, it sells beer, Indonesian coffee and countless different tea blends.

DE JAREN

Nieuwe Doelenstraat 20 ⓣ 020 625 5771, ⓦ cafedejaren.nl. Daily 9.30am–1am, Fri & Sat until 2am. MAP PP.34–35, POCKET MAP B14

One of the grandest of the grand cafés, overlooking the Amstel next to the university, with three floors and two terraces. A great place to nurse the Sunday papers. It serves reasonably priced food too, and there's a good salad bar.

PUCCINI

Staalstraat 21 ⓣ 020 620 8458, ⓦ puccini.nl. Mon–Fri 8.30am–6pm, Sat & Sun 10am–6pm. MAP PP.34–35, POCKET MAP C14

Lovely café that serves delicious salads, sandwiches and pastries, a few doors down from its sister chocolate shop (see p.47).

VAN BEEREN

Koningstraat 54 ⓣ 020 622 2329, ⓦ eetcafevanbeeren.nl. Daily 5pm–1am. MAP PP.34–35, POCKET MAP D12

This *eetcafé* serves a satisfying mixture of Dutch staples and modern European fare in relaxed surroundings.

Restaurants

BIRD

Zeedijk 77 ⓣ 020 420 6289, ⓦ thai-bird.nl. Daily 1–10pm. MAP PP.34–35, POCKET MAP D11

This inexpensive and authentic Thai canteen is always packed, and rightly so. Its big brother across the road serves much the same food in slightly more upscale surroundings.

BLAUW AAN DE WAL

Oudezijds Achterburgwal 99 ⓣ 020 330 2257, ⓦ blauwaandewal.com. Tues–Sat 6–11pm. MAP PP.34–35, POCKET MAP C12

A haven of calm, situated down an alley in the heart of the Red Light District, with tremendous French-Dutch food.

DE COMPAGNON

Guldenhandsteeg 17 ⓣ 020 620 4225, ⓦ decompagnon.nl. Mon–Fri noon–2pm & 6–10pm, Sat 6–10pm. MAP PP.34–35, POCKET MAP C11

Excellent French cuisine is on offer here at this traditional restaurant. First-rate wine cellar too – and knowledgeable staff to help. Reservations advised. Mains average €25.

HEMELSE MODDER

Oude Waal 11 ⓣ 020 624 3203, ⓦ hemelsemodder.nl. Daily 6–10pm. MAP PP.34–35, POCKET MAP D12

Welcoming Dutch restaurant serving tasty meat and fish dishes at reasonable prices in an informal atmosphere. The name "heavenly mud" refers to the dark and white chocolate dessert with vanilla cream.

LUCIUS

Spuistraat 247 ⓣ 020 624 1831, ⓦ lucius.nl. Daily 5pm–midnight. MAP PP.34–35, POCKET MAP A13

This bistro-style restaurant, with its high-varnish wooden panelling, is one of the best fish restaurants in town. The lemon sole, when it's on the menu, is particularly excellent. Attracts an older clientele. Mains €30, a tad less for the daily special.

MAPPA

Nes 59 ⓣ 020 528 9170, ⓦ www.mappa.nl. Tues–Sat 6–10pm. MAP PP.34–35, POCKET MAP B13

Classic Italian with inventive twists, incorporating good home-made pasta dishes and excellent service in an unpretentious, modern setting.

NAM KEE

Zeedijk 111–113 ⓣ 020 624 3470, ⓦ namkee.net. Daily noon–11pm. MAP PP.34–35, POCKET MAP C12

Arguably the best of a number of inexpensive Chinese diners along this stretch of the Zeedijk.

SAMPURNA

Singel 498 ⓣ 020 625 3264, ⓦ sampurna.com. Daily noon–11pm. MAP PP.34–35, POCKET MAP A14

One of the city's favourite Asian restaurants, the *Sampurna* has been serving classic Indonesian cuisine for several decades. Saté skewers are under €10, main dishes around €20–25.

DE JAREN

DE SILVEREN SPIEGEL

Kattengat 4 020 624 6589, desilverenspiegel.com. Mon & Tues 9am–5.30pm, Wed–Sat 9am–10pm, Sun 9.30am–10pm. MAP PP.34–35, POCKET MAP B10

This long-established restaurant, "The Silver Mirror", is one of Amsterdam's best, offering a delicately balanced menu of Dutch dishes. Tasting menus range from €40 to €115.

VAN KERKWIJK

Nes 41 020 620 3316, www.caferestaurantvankerkwijk.nl. Daily 11am–1am. MAP PP.34–35, POCKET MAP B12

This restaurant serves steaks, fish and so forth, from an ever-changing unwritten menu that is heroically memorized by the attentive waiting staff. Good food, and cheap too – mains from €15.

Bars

DE BEKEERDE SUSTER

Kloveniersburgwal 6 020 423 0112, debekeerdesuster.nl. Mon–Thurs 3pm–1am, Fri & Sat noon–2am, Sun noon–midnight. MAP PP.34–35, POCKET MAP C12

Don't waste your time in the unappealing drinkeries of the Red Light District proper; this place is a few steps away and offers home-brewed beer, good food and a fun atmosphere.

BELGIQUE

Gravenstraat 2 020 625 1974, cafe-belgique.nl. Daily 3pm–1am. MAP PP.34–35, POCKET MAP B12

Tiny bar behind the Nieuwe Kerk that serves up Belgian brews alongside Trappist cheese.

BUBBLES & WINES

Nes 37 020 422 3318, bubblesandwines.com. Mon–Sat 3.30pm–1am, Sun 2–9pm. MAP PP.34–35, POCKET MAP B12

Over fifty wines by the glass in this elegant wine and champagne bar. In-the-know staff will help you decide.

DE BUURVROUW

St Pieterspoortsteeg 29 020 625 9654, debuurvrouw.nl. Mon–Thurs & Sun 10pm–3am, Fri & Sat 10pm–4am. MAP PP.34–35, POCKET MAP B13

Take a walk on the wild side at this dark, noisy bar where the music throbs way into the early hours. In the heart of the Red Light District – and it shows.

CAFÉ DE DOKTER

Roozenboomsteeg 4 020 626 4427, cafe-de-dokter.nl. Tues–Sat 4pm–1am. MAP PP.34–35, POCKET MAP A13

Typical café with stained glass and ancient furnishings. Liqueurs fill the shelves behind the tiny bar, and the *ossenworst* (smoked sausage) is delicious.

DE DRIE FLESCHJES

Gravenstraat 18 020 624 8443, dedriefleschjes.nl. Mon–Sat 2–8.30pm, Sun 3–8pm. MAP PP.34–35, POCKET MAP B12

Tasting house for spirits and liqueurs. Clients tend to be well heeled or well soused (or both).

DE ENGELBEWAARDER

Kloveniersburgwal 59 020 625 3772, cafe-de-engelbewaarder.nl. Mon–Thurs 11am–1am, Fri & Sat 11am–3am, Sun 11am–1am. MAP PP.34–35, POCKET MAP C13

BUBBLES & WINES

Once the meeting place of Amsterdam's bookish types, this is still known as a literary café. It's relaxed and informal, with live jazz on Sunday afternoons.

HOPPE

Spui 18 ☎ 020 420 4420, ⓦ cafehoppe.com. Daily 8am–1am, Fri & Sat until 2am. MAP P.34–35, POCKET MAP A13

One of Amsterdam's oldest and best-known bars, frequented by the city's businessfolk on their wayward way home. Summer is especially good, when the throngs spill out onto the street.

IN DE WILDEMAN

Kolksteeg 3 ☎ 020 638 2348, ⓦ indewildeman.nl. Mon–Thurs noon–1am, Fri & Sat noon–2am. MAP PP.34–35, POCKET MAP B11

This lovely old-fashioned bar is housed in a former distillery and offers a huge range of beers (250 and counting) from around the world. A peaceful escape from the loud, tacky shops of nearby Nieuwendijk.

IN 'T AEPJEN

Zeedijk 1 ☎ 020 428 8291. Daily noon–1am. MAP PP.34–35, POCKET MAP C11

A bar since the days when Zeedijk was the haunt of sailors on the razzle, and still one of the city centre's best watering holes. Get a plate of cheese or sausage to help the ale go down.

LUXEMBOURG

Spui 24 ☎ 020 620 6264, ⓦ luxembourg.nl. Daily 9am–1am. MAP PP.34–35, POCKET MAP A13

Crowded, trendy grand café with a long and deep bar, a good selection of snacks, and possibly the best hamburgers in town.

WYNAND FOCKINK

Pijlsteeg 31 Daily 3–9pm. MAP PP.34–35, POCKET MAP B12

Intimate bar hidden just behind the *Krasnapolsky* hotel off The Dam. It offers a vast range of its own flavoured *jenevers* that used to be distilled down the street.

LUXEMBOURG

Clubs and venues

BITTERZOET

Spuistraat 2 ☎ 020 421 2318, ⓦ bitterzoet .com. Daily 8pm–3am. MAP PP.34–35, POCKET MAP B11

Spacious but cosy two-floored bar and theatre hosting a mixed bag of events: DJ sets, live gigs featuring European indie bands, plus occasional poetry and film nights.

CLUB NL

Nieuwezijds Voorburgwal 169 ☎ 020 622 7510, ⓦ clubnl.nl. Daily 10pm–3am, Fri & Sat until 4am. MAP PP.34–35, POCKET MAP A12

What used to be the capital's first lounge bar turned into a stylish house club, frequented by designer-clad young things.

WINSTON KINGDOM

Warmoesstraat 131 ☎ 020 623 1380, ⓦ winston.nl. Daily 9pm–3am, Fri & Sat from 11pm. MAP PP.34–35, POCKET MAP C12

Underground venue in the heart of the Red Light District, hosting everything from DJ nights to band competitions and themed parties.

The Grachtengordel

The Grachtengordel, or "girdle of canals", reaches right round the city centre and is without doubt the most charming part of Amsterdam, its lattice of olive-green waterways and dinky humpback bridges overlooked by street upon street of handsome seventeenth-century canal houses. It's a subtle cityscape – full of surprises, with a bizarre carving here, an unusual facade there, but it is the district's overall atmosphere that appeals rather than any specific sight, with the exception of the Anne Frank Huis. There's no obvious walking route around the Grachtengordel, and you may prefer to wander around as the mood takes you, but the description we've given below goes from north to south, taking in all the highlights on the way. On all three of the main canals – Herengracht, Keizersgracht and Prinsengracht – street numbers begin in the north and increase as you go south.

BROUWERSGRACHT

MAP PP.54–55, POCKET MAP C1–D2

Running east to west along the northern edge of the three main canals is leafy, memorably picturesque **Brouwersgracht**. Originally, Brouwersgracht lay at the edge of Amsterdam's great harbour with easy access to the sea. This was where ships returning from the East unloaded their silks and spices and breweries flourished here too, capitalizing on their ready access to fresh water. Today, the harbour bustle has moved elsewhere, and the warehouses, with their distinctive spout-neck gables and shuttered windows, which were formerly used for the delivery and dispatch of goods by pulley from the canal below, have been converted into ritzy apartments. These have proved particularly attractive to actors and film producers. There are handsome merchants' houses here as well, plus moored houseboats and a string of quaint little swing bridges. Restaurants have sprung up here too, including one of the city's best, *De Belhamel* (see p.66).

BROUWERSGRACHT

The canals

The canals of the Grachtengordel were dug in the seventeenth century in order to extend the boundaries of a city no longer able to accommodate its burgeoning population. Increasing the area of the city from two to seven square kilometres was a monumental task, and the conditions imposed by the council were strict. The three main waterways – Herengracht, Keizersgracht and Prinsengracht – were set aside for the residences and businesses of the richer and more influential Amsterdam merchants, while the radial cross-streets were reserved for more modest artisans' homes; meanwhile, immigrants, newly arrived to cash in on Amsterdam's booming economy, were assigned, albeit informally, the Jodenhoek (see p.80) and the Jordaan (see p.72). In the Grachtengordel, everyone, even the wealthiest merchant, had to comply with a set of detailed planning regulations. In particular, the council prescribed the size of each building plot – the frontage was set at thirty feet, the depth two hundred – and although there was a degree of tinkering, the end result was the loose conformity you can see today: tall, narrow residences, whose individualism is mainly restricted to the stylistic permutations amongst the **gables**.

The earliest gables, dating from the early seventeenth century, are the so-called **crow-stepped** gables, which were largely superseded by **neck gables** and **bell gables**, both named for the shape of the gable top. Some are embellished, some aren't, many have decorative cornices and the fanciest – which mostly date from the eighteenth century – sport full-scale balustrades. The plainest gables belong to the warehouses, where deep-arched and shuttered windows line up on either side of the loft doors that were originally (and often still are) used for loading and unloading goods winched by pulley from the street down below.

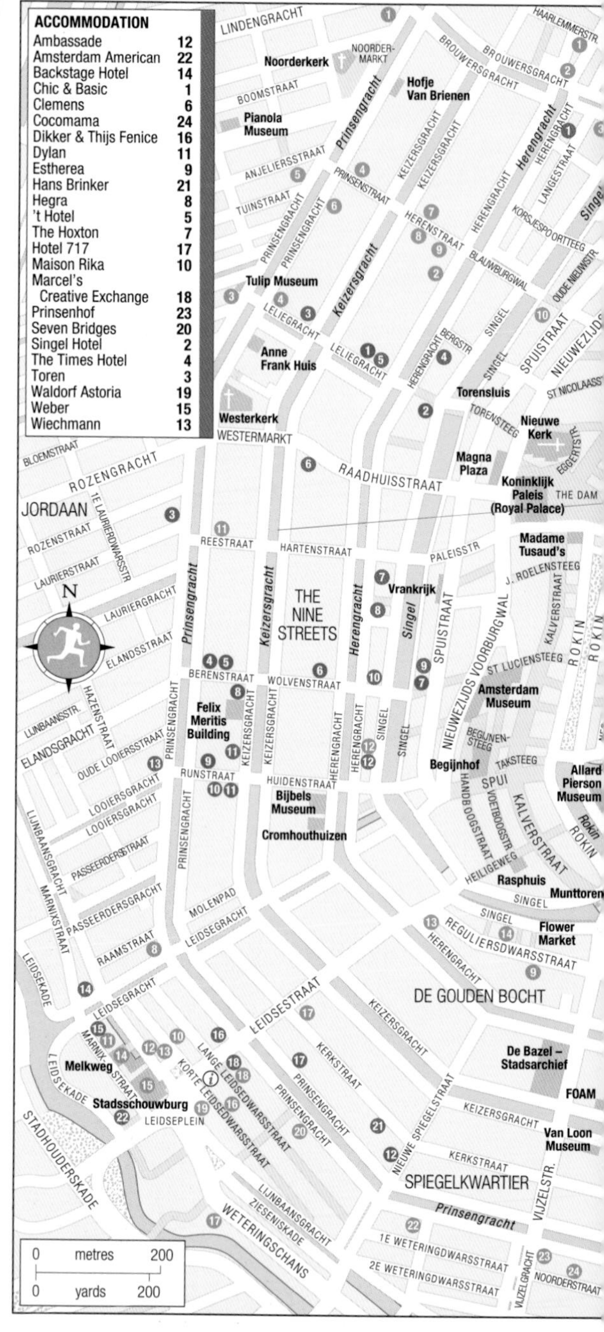
ACCOMMODATION
Ambassade 12
Amsterdam American 22
Backstage Hotel 14
Chic & Basic 1
Clemens 6
Cocomama 24
Dikker & Thijs Fenice 16
Dylan 11
Estherea 9
Hans Brinker 21
Hegra 8
't Hotel 5
The Hoxton 7
Hotel 717 17
Maison Rika 10
Marcel's Creative Exchange 18
Prinsenhof 23
Seven Bridges 20
Singel Hotel 2
The Times Hotel 4
Toren 3
Waldorf Astoria 19
Weber 15
Wiechmann 13
LINDENGRACHT
HAARLEMMERSTR.
Noorderkerk
NOORDERMARKT
BROUWERSGRACHT
Hofje Van Brienen
BOOMSTRAAT
Pianola Museum
Prinsengracht
Herengracht
ANJELIERSSTRAAT
PRINSENSTRAAT
KEIZERSGRACHT
LANGESTRAAT
TUINSTRAAT
HERENSTRAAT
KORSJESPOORTTEEG
BLAUWBURGWAL
OUDE NIEUWSTR.
Tulip Museum
Keizersgracht
LELIEGRACHT
SINGEL
SPUISTRAAT
NIEUWEZIJDS
Anne Frank Huis
BERGSTR
Torensluis
ST NICOLAASSTR.
TORENSTEEG
Nieuwe Kerk
Westerkerk
WESTERMARKT
Magna Plaza
EGGERTSTR.
BLOEMSTRAAT
ROZENGRACHT
RAADHUISSTRAAT
Koninklijk Paleis (Royal Palace)
THE DAM
JORDAAN
1E LAURIERDWARSSTR
REESTRAAT
HARTENSTRAAT
Madame Tusaud's
ROZENSTRAAT
PALEISSTR
LAURIERSTRAAT
J. ROELENSTEEG
N
LAURIERGRACHT
Vrankrijk
THE NINE STREETS
Singel
KALVERSTRAAT
ROKIN
NIEUWEZIJDS VOORBURGWAL
ELANDSSTRAAT
BERENSTRAAT
WOLVENSTRAAT
ST LUCIENSTEEG
HAZENSTRAAT
Amsterdam Museum
Felix Meritis Building
LIJNBAANSSTR.
ELANDSGRACHT
OUDE LOOIERSSTRAAT
BEGIJNENSTEEG
Begijnhof
TAKSTEEG
RUNSTRAAT
HUIDENSTRAAT
SPUI
Allard Pierson Museum
Bijbels Museum
LOOIERSGRACHT
Cromhouthuizen
HANDBOOGSTRAAT
VOETBOOGSTR.
LIJNBAANSGRACHT
PASSEERDERSSTRAAT
HEILIGEWEG
Rasphuis
MARNIXSTRAAT
Munttoren
MOLENPAD
PASSEERDERSGRACHT
LEIDSEGRACHT
Flower Market
REGULIERSDWARSSTRAAT
RAAMSTRAAT
LEIDSEKADE
DE GOUDEN BOCHT
LEIDSESTRAAT
Melkweg
LANGE LEIDSEDWARSSTRAAT
KERKSTRAAT
De Bazel – Stadsarchief
KORTE LEIDSEDWARSSTRAAT
Stadsschouwburg
LEIDSEPLEIN
FOAM
Van Loon Museum
STADHOUDERSKADE
NIEUWE SPIEGELSTRAAT
SPIEGELKWARTIER
VIJZELSTR.
WETERINGSCHANS
ZIESENISKADE
1E WETERINGDWARSSTRAAT
2E WETERINGDWARSSTRAAT
VIJZELGRACHT
NOORDERSTRAAT
0 metres 200
0 yards 200

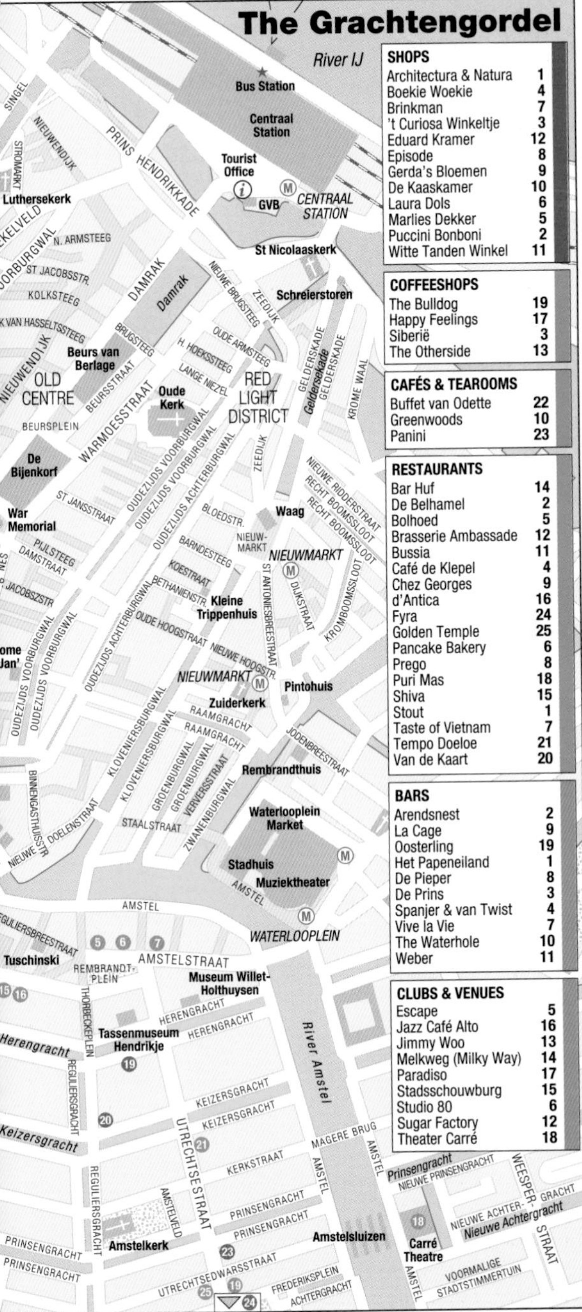
The Grachtengordel
SHOPS
Architectura & Natura 1
Boekie Woekie 4
Brinkman 7
't Curiosa Winkeltje 3
Eduard Kramer 12
Episode 8
Gerda's Bloemen 9
De Kaaskamer 10
Laura Dols 6
Marlies Dekker 5
Puccini Bonboni 2
Witte Tanden Winkel 11
COFFEESHOPS
The Bulldog 19
Happy Feelings 17
Siberië 3
The Otherside 13
CAFÉS & TEAROOMS
Buffet van Odette 22
Greenwoods 10
Panini 23
RESTAURANTS
Bar Huf 14
De Belhamel 2
Bolhoed 5
Brasserie Ambassade 12
Bussia 11
Café de Klepel 4
Chez Georges 9
d'Antica 16
Fyra 24
Golden Temple 25
Pancake Bakery 6
Prego 8
Puri Mas 18
Shiva 15
Stout 1
Taste of Vietnam 7
Tempo Doeloe 21
Van de Kaart 20
BARS
Arendsnest 2
La Cage 9
Oosterling 19
Het Papeneiland 1
De Pieper 8
De Prins 3
Spanjer & van Twist 4
Vive la Vie 7
The Waterhole 10
Weber 11
CLUBS & VENUES
Escape 5
Jazz Café Alto 16
Jimmy Woo 13
Melkweg (Milky Way) 14
Paradiso 17
Stadsschouwburg 15
Studio 80 6
Sugar Factory 12
Theater Carré 18
River IJ
Bus Station
Centraal Station
Tourist Office
GVB
CENTRAAL STATION
St Nicolaaskerk
Schreierstoren
PRINS HENDRIKKADE
SINGEL
NIEUWENDIJK
STROMARKT
Luthersekerk
N. ARMSTEEG
ST JACOBSSTR.
KOLKSTEEG
DAMRAK
Damrak
NIEUWE BRUGSTEEG
ZEEDIJK
OUDE ARMSTEEG
H. HOEKSSTEEG
LANGE NIEZEL
BRUGSTEEG
BEURSSTRAAT
Beurs van Berlage
OLD CENTRE
RED LIGHT DISTRICT
Oude Kerk
BEURSPLEIN
WARMOESSTRAAT
GELDERSKADE
Geldersekade
KROME WAAL
De Bijenkorf
ST JANSSTRAAT
War Memorial
OUDEZIJDS VOORBURGWAL
OUDEZIJDS ACHTERBURGWAL
BLOEDSTR.
Waag
NIEUWMARKT
NIEUWE RIDDERSTRAAT
RECHT BOOMSSLOOT
BARNDESTEEG
KOESTRAAT
BETHANIENSTR.
Kleine Trippenhuis
ST ANTONIESBREESTRAAT
DIJKSTRAAT
KROMBOOMSSLOOT
PIJLSTEEG
DAMSTRAAT
OUDE HOOGSTRAAT
NIEUWE HOOGSTR.
Pintohuis
Zuiderkerk
RAAMGRACHT
JODENBREESTRAAT
Rembrandthuis
KLOVENIERSBURGWAL
GROENBURGWAL
VERWERSSTRAAT
ZWANENBURGWAL
STAALSTRAAT
BINNENGASTHUISSTR
DOELENSTRAAT
Waterlooplein Market
Stadhuis
Muziektheater
AMSTEL
WATERLOOPLEIN
Tuschinski
REMBRANDTPLEIN
AMSTELSTRAAT
Museum Willet-Holthuysen
THORBECKEPLEIN
HERENGRACHT
Herengracht
Tassenmuseum Hendrikje
River Amstel
REGULIERSGRACHT
KEIZERSGRACHT
Keizersgracht
UTRECHTSESTRAAT
MAGERE BRUG
KERKSTRAAT
Prinsengracht
NIEUWE PRINSENGRACHT
WEESPERSTRAAT
PRINSENGRACHT
AMSTELVELD
Amstelkerk
Amstelsluizen
Carré Theatre
NIEUWE ACHTERGRACHT
Nieuwe Achtergracht
UTRECHTSEDWARSSTRAAT
FREDERIKSPLEIN
ACHTERGRACHT
VOORMALIGE STADTSTIMMERTUIN

NOORDERKERK

Noorderkermarkt ⓣ020 626 6436, ⓦnoorderkerk.org. Mon 10.30am–12.30pm, Sat 11am–1pm. Free. MAP PP.54–55, POCKET MAP C2

Prolific architect Hendrik de Keyser's last creation, finished two years after his death in 1623, this bulky brick building represented a radical departure from the conventional church designs of the time, having a symmetrical Greek-cross floor plan, with four arms radiating out from a steepled centre. Uncompromisingly dour, it proclaimed the serious intent of the Calvinists who worshipped here, its pulpit placed in the centre as a complete break with the Catholic past.

NOORDERMARKT

MAP PP.54–55, POCKET MAP C2

In the shadow of the Noorderkerk, the **Noordermarkt** is a substantial albeit rather unimpressive square, whose main item of interest is a statue of three figures bound to each other, representing a tribute to the bloody Jordaanoproer riot of 1934. The riot was part of a successful campaign to stop the government cutting unemployment benefit during the Depression; you'll find the statue just in front of the church's door. On Saturday's (9am–4pm) the square hosts one of Amsterdam's best **markets** – the farmers' market, **Boerenmarkt**.

HOFJE VAN BRIENEN

Prinsengracht 85–133 Mon–Fri 6am–6pm & Sat 6am–2pm. Free. MAP PP.54–55, POCKET MAP C2

On the east side of Prinsengracht, opposite the Noorderkerk (see above), this brown-brick courtyard was built as an almshouse (*hofje*) in 1804 by Aernout van Brienen. A well-to-do merchant, Van Brienen had locked himself in his own strongroom by accident and, in a panic, he vowed to build a *hofje* if he was rescued: he was and he did. The plaque inside the complex doesn't give much of the game away: it is simply inscribed with "For the relief and shelter of those in need."

LELIEGRACHT

MAP PP.54–55, POCKET MAP C3

Leliegracht leads east off Prinsengracht, and is one of the tiny radial canals that cut across the Grachtengordel. It holds one of the city's finest Art Nouveau buildings, a tall and

THE HOFJE VAN BRIENEN

striking building at the Leliegracht-Keizersgracht junction designed by Gerrit van Arkel in 1905. It was originally the headquarters of a life insurance company – hence the two mosaics with angels recommending policies to bemused earthlings.

ANNE FRANK HUIS

Prinsengracht 263–267 ⓣ 020 556 7100, ⓦ annefrank.org. Daily: April to Oct 9am–10pm; Nov to March 9am–7pm (Sat till 9pm); closed Yom Kippur. €9, 10- to 17-year-olds €4.50, under-9s free. Queues can be long, and from 9am–3.30pm the museum is only open to those who have booked online. MAP PP.54–55, POCKET MAP C3

Easily the city's most visited sight, the **Anne Frank Huis** is where the young diarist and her family hid from the Germans during World War II. Since the posthumous publication of her diaries, Anne Frank has become extraordinarily famous, in the first instance for recording the iniquities of the Holocaust, and latterly as a symbol of the fight against oppression and in particular racism. The family spent over two years in hiding here between 1942 and 1944, but were eventually betrayed and dispatched to Westerbork – the transit camp in the north of the country where most Dutch Jews were processed before being moved to Belsen or Auschwitz. Of the eight souls hidden in the annexe, only Otto Frank survived; Anne and her sister died of typhus within a short time of each other in Belsen, just one week before the German surrender.

Anne Frank's **diary** was among the few things left behind in the annexe. It was retrieved by one of the people who had helped the Franks and handed to Anne's father on his return from Auschwitz; he later decided to publish it. Since its appearance in 1947, it has been constantly in print and has sold millions of copies.

ENTRANCE TO SECRET ANNEXE AT THE ANNE FRANK HUIS

Despite being so popular, the house has managed to preserve a sense of intimacy, a poignant witness to the personal nature of the Franks' sufferings. The rooms they occupied for two years have been left much the same as they were during the war, albeit without the furniture – down to the movie star pin-ups in Anne's bedroom and the marks on the wall recording the children's heights. Film clips of the family and the Holocaust give the background. Anne Frank was one of about one hundred thousand Dutch Jews who died during World War II, and her home provides one of the most enduring testaments to its horrors.

WESTERKERK

Prinsengracht 281 Church ⓣ 020 624 7766, ⓦ westerkerk.nl; Mon–Fri 10am–3pm plus April–Oct Sat 11am–3pm; free. **Tower** ⓣ 020 689 2565, ⓦ westertorenamsterdam.nl; daily: April–Sept 10am–8pm, Oct 10am–6pm; €7.50. MAP PP.54–55, POCKET MAP C3

Trapped in her house, Anne Frank liked to listen to the bells of the neighbouring **Westerkerk**, until they were taken away to be melted down for the German war effort. The church still dominates the district, its 85m tower – without question Amsterdam's finest – soaring graciously above its surroundings. The church was designed by Hendrick de Keyser and completed in 1631 as part of the general enlargement of the city, but whereas the exterior is all studied elegance, the interior is bare and plain.

WESTERMARKT

MAP PP.54–55, POCKET MAP C3

Westermarkt, an open square in the shadow of the Westerkerk, possesses two evocative memorials. At the back of the church, beside Keizersgracht, are the three pink granite triangles (one each for the past, present and future) of the **Homomonument**, the world's first memorial to persecuted gays and lesbians, commemorating all those who died at the hands of the Germans. It was designed by Karin Daan and recalls the pink triangles the Nazis made homosexuals sew onto their clothes during World War II.

Nearby, on the south side of the church by Prinsengracht, is a small but beautifully crafted **statue** of Anne Frank by the modern Dutch sculptor Mari Andriessen.

WESTERMARKT TO LEIDSEGRACHT – THE NINE STREETS

MAP PP.54–55, POCKET MAP C3–C5

Between Westermarkt and Leidsegracht, the main canals are intercepted by a trio of cross-streets, which are themselves divided into shorter streets mostly named after animals whose pelts were once used in the district's tanning industry. There's Reestraat (Deer Street), Hartenstraat (Hart), Berenstraat (Bear) and Wolvenstraat (Wolf), not to mention Huidenstraat (Street of Hides) and Runstraat – a "run" being a bark used in tanning. The tanners are long gone and today these are eminently appealing shopping streets, known collectively as **De Negen Straatjes** (The Nine Streets).

FELIX MERITIS BUILDING

Keizersgracht 324 ⓣ 020 626 2321, ⓦ felixmeritis.nl. MAP PP.54–55, POCKET MAP C4

THE FELIX MERITIS BUILDING

STADSSCHOUWBURG

A Neoclassical monolith of 1787, this mansion was built to house the artistic and scientific activities of the eponymous society, which was the cultural focus of the city's upper crust for nearly a hundred years. Oddly enough, it later became the headquarters of the Dutch Communist Party, but they sold it to the council who now lease it to the Felix Meritis Foundation for experimental and avant-garde art workshops, conferences, discussions and debates.

BIJBELS MUSEUM

Herengracht 366–368 ⓣ 020 624 2436, ⓦ bijbelsmuseum.nl. Tues–Sun 11am–5pm. €8.50. MAP PP.54–55, POCKET MAP C4

The graceful and commanding **Cromhouthuizen**, at Herengracht 364–370, is comprised of four matching stone mansions, built in the 1660s for one of Amsterdam's wealthy merchant families, the Cromhouts. Two of these mansions now accommodate the **Bijbels Museum**, one of the city's more unusual museums, holding a splendid selection of old Bibles, including the first Dutch-language Bible ever printed, dating from 1477. Here also is a small display on the Cromhout family; a café; a small and formal garden; an antique kitchen; and a series of idiosyncratic models of Solomon's Temple and the Jewish Tabernacle, alongside a scattering of archeological finds from Palestine and Egypt.

LEIDSEPLEIN

MAP PP.54–55, POCKET MAP C5

Lying on the edge of the Grachtengordel, **Leidseplein** is a bustling hub of city nightlife. The square once marked the end of the road in from Leiden and, as horse-drawn traffic was banned from the centre long ago, it was here that the Dutch left their horses and carts – a sort of equine car park. Today, it's quite the opposite: continual traffic made up of trams, bikes, cars and pedestrians gives the place a frenetic feel, and the surrounding side streets are jammed with bars, restaurants and clubs in a bright jumble of jutting signs and neon lights. On a good night, Leidseplein can be Amsterdam at its carefree, exuberant best.

STADSSCHOUWBURG

Leidseplein 26 ⓣ 020 624 2311, ⓦ stadsschouwburgamsterdam.nl. MAP PP.54–55, POCKET MAP B5

Leidseplein holds the grandiose **Stadsschouwburg**, a neo-Renaissance edifice dating from 1894, which was so widely criticized for its clumsy vulgarity that the city council of the day temporarily withheld the money for decorating the interior. Home to the National Ballet and Opera until the Muziektheater (see p.82) was completed on Waterlooplein in 1986, it is now used for theatre, dance and music performances. It also functions as the spot where the Ajax football team gather on the balcony to wave to the crowds whenever they win anything, as they often do.

LEIDSESTRAAT

MAP PP.54–55, POCKET MAP C5

Heading northeast from Leidseplein, **Leidsestraat** is a busy shopping street that leads across the three main canals up towards the Singel and the flower market (see p.63).

SPIEGELKWARTIER

MAP PP.54–55, POCKET MAP C6

One block east of Leidsestraat is **Nieuwe Spiegelstraat**, an appealing mixture of shops, stores and corner cafés that extends south into Spiegelgracht to form the Spiegelkwartier – home to the pricey end of Amsterdam's antiques trade.

DE GOUDEN BOCHT

MAP PP.54–55, POCKET MAP D5

Nieuwe Spiegelstraat meets the elegant sweep of Herengracht near the west end of the so-called De Gouden Bocht (the **Golden Bend**), where the canal is overlooked by double-fronted mansions – some of the most opulent dwellings in the city. Most of these houses were remodelled in the late seventeenth and eighteenth centuries. Characteristically, they have double stairways leading to the entrance, underneath which the small door was for the servants, while up above, the majority of the houses are topped off by the ornamental cornices that were fashionable at the time. Classical references are common, both in form – pediments, columns and pilasters – and decoration, from scrolls and vases through to geometric patterns inspired by ancient Greece.

DE BAZEL – THE STADSARCHIEF

Vijzelstraat 32 ⓣ 020 251 1511, ⓦ amsterdam.nl/stadsarchief; Tues–Fri 10am–5pm, Sat & Sun noon–5pm; Free.
MAP PP.54–55, POCKET MAP D6

DE BAZEL – THE STADSARCHIEF

De Bazel, one of Amsterdam's weirdest and most incongruous buildings, stretches south down Vijzelstraat from Herengracht – you can't miss its looming, geometrical brickwork. Dating to the 1920s, this whopper of a structure was designed by the architect **Karel de Bazel** (1869–1923), whose devotion to theosophy formed and framed its design. Indeed, every facet of Bazel's building reflects the theosophical desire for order and balance, from the (faded) pink and yellow brickwork of the exterior (representing male and female respectively) to the repeated use of interior motifs drawn from the Middle East, the source of much of the cult's spiritual inspiration. The building started out as the headquarters of a Dutch shipping company, the **Nederlandsche Handelsmaatschappij**, but is now home to a conference centre and the **Stadsarchief**, the vast city archives. A rotated selection of documents and photographs drawn from the archives is displayed in De Bazel's richly decorated Art Deco **Schatkamer** (Treasury).

MUSEUM VAN LOON

Keizersgracht 672 ⓣ 020 624 5255, ⓦ museumvanloon.nl. Daily 10am–5pm. €9. MAP PP.54–55, POCKET MAP D6

The **Museum Van Loon** boasts the finest accessible canal house interior in Amsterdam. Built in 1672, and first occupied by the artist and pupil of Rembrandt, Ferdinand Bol, the house has been returned to something akin to its eighteenth-century appearance, with acres of wood panelling and fancy stucco work. Look out also for the ornate copper balustrade on the staircase, into which is worked the name "Van Hagen-Trip" (after a one-time owner of the house); the Van Loons later filled the spaces between the letters with iron curlicues to prevent their children falling through. The top-floor landing has several paintings sporting Roman figures, and one of the bedrooms – the "painted room" – is decorated with a Romantic painting of Italy, a favourite motif in Amsterdam from around 1750 to 1820. The oddest items are the fake bedroom doors: the eighteenth-century owners were so keen to avoid any lack of symmetry that they camouflaged the real bedroom doors and created imitation, decorative doors in the "correct" position instead.

FOAM

Keizersgracht 609 ⓣ 020 551 6500, ⓦ www.foam.org. Daily 10am–6pm, Thurs & Fri until 9pm. €10. MAP PP.54–55, POCKET MAP D5

In a large and thoroughly refurbished old canal house, Amsterdam's leading photography museum **FOAM** (short for Fotografiemuseum) is achingly fashionable, its temporary exhibitions – of which there are usually four at any one time – featuring the best (or most obscure) of contemporary photographers. FOAM prides itself on its internationalism, though it does give space to famous or up-and-coming Dutch photographers like Carel Willink, Frido Troost and Otto Kaan. FOAM also offers guided, walk-through tours and photography workshops, both of which are extremely popular.

TASSENMUSEUM HENDRIKJE (PURSE & BAG MUSEUM)

Herengracht 573 020 524 6452, tassenmuseum.nl. Daily 10am–5pm. €12.50. MAP PP.54–55, POCKET MAP E5

This delightful museum holds a superb collection of handbags, pouches, wallets, bags and purses from medieval times onwards, exhibited on three floors of a grand old mansion. The collection begins on the top floor with a curious miscellany of items from the sixteenth to the nineteenth centuries. The next floor down focuses on the twentieth century, with several beautiful Art Nouveau handbags, while the final floor is given over to temporary displays.

MUSEUM WILLET-HOLTHUYSEN

Herengracht 605 020 523 1822, willetholthuysen.nl. Mon–Fri 10am–5pm, Sat & Sun 11am–5pm. €9. MAP PP.54–55, POCKET MAP E5

The coal-trading Holthuysen family occupied this elegant, mansion until the last of the line, Louisa Willet-Holthuysen, gifted her home and its contents to the city in 1895. The most striking room is the **Men's Parlour**, which has been returned to its original nineteenth-century Rococo appearance – a flashy and ornate style that the Dutch merchants of the day regarded as the epitome of refinement and good taste. The house also displays a small but tasteful collection of fine and applied art assembled by Louisa's husband, Abraham Willet.

THE AMSTEL AND THE MAGERE BRUG

MAP PP.54–55, POCKET MAP E5–G9 & F6

The Grachtengordel comes to an abrupt halt at the River Amstel. The **Magere Brug** (Skinny Bridge), spanning the Amstel at the end of Kerkstraat, is the most famous and arguably the cutest of the city's many swing bridges. Legend has it that this bridge, which dates back to about 1670, replaced an even older and skinnier version, originally built by two sisters who lived on either side of the river and were fed up with having to walk so far to see each other.

AMSTELSLUIZEN

MAP PP.54–55, POCKET MAP F6

The **Amstelsluizen** – or Amstel locks – are closed every night when the council begins the process of sluicing out the canals. A huge pumping station

THE MUSEUM WILLET-HOLTHUYSEN

BLOEMENMARKT

on an island out to the east of the city then starts to pump fresh water from the IJsselmeer into the canal system; similar locks on the west side of the city are left open for the surplus to flow into the IJ and, from there, out to sea. The watery content of the canals is thus regularly refreshed – though, what with all the shopping trolleys and rusty bikes, the water is only appealing as long as you're not actually in it.

THE AMSTELVELD AND REGULIERSGRACHT

MAP PP.54–55, POCKET MAP D5

Doubling back from the Amstelsluizen, turn left along the north side of Prinsengracht and you soon reach the **Amstelveld**, where the Monday **flower market** sells flowers and plants, and is much less of a scrum than the Bloemenmarkt (see p.below). Adjacent **Reguliersgracht** is one of the three surviving radial canals that cut across the Grachtengordel, its dainty humpback bridges and dark waters overlooked by charming seventeenth- and eighteenth-century canal houses.

REMBRANDTPLEIN

MAP PP.54–55, POCKET MAP E5

Rembrandtplein may not be Amsterdam at its most alluring, but it is one of the city's nightlife centres, its bevy of restaurants and bars rammed at weekends. Formerly the city's butter market, the square took its present name in 1876 after it had acquired a statue of Rembrandt, a rather prim and proper affair that seems particularly appealing to passing seagulls. The statue now overlooks the life-size, bronze figures of **Nachtwacht 3D**, a sort of replica of Rembrandt's *Night Watch* painting (see p.101), the work of two Russians – Alexander Taratynov and Mikhail Dronov.

THE MUNTTOREN AND BLOEMENMARKT (FLOWER MARKET)

MAP PP.54–55, POCKET MAP D5

Tiny Muntplein is dominated by the **Munttoren**, an imposing fifteenth-century tower that was once part of the old city wall. Later, the tower was adopted as the municipal mint – hence its name – and celebrated Amsterdam architect Hendrik de Keyser, in one of his last commissions, added a flashy spire in 1620. A few metres away, the floating Bloemenmarkt, or **flower market** (daily 9am–5pm, some stalls close on Sun), extends along the southern bank of the Singel. Popular with locals and tourists alike, the market is one of the main suppliers of flowers to central Amsterdam, but its blooms and bulbs now share stall space with souvenir clogs, garden gnomes and similar tat.

Shops

ARCHITECTURA & NATURA

Leliegracht 22 020 623 6186, www.architectura.nl. Core hours: Mon noon–6pm, Tues–Sat 10am–6pm & Sun 1–5pm. MAP PP.54–55, POCKET MAP A11

Outstanding specialist bookshop that more than knows its onions when it comes to architecture, landscape architecture and natural history. Around half of the stock is in English, too.

BOEKIE WOEKIE

Berenstraat 16 020 639 0507, boewoe.home.xs4all.nl. Daily noon–6pm. MAP PP.54–55, POCKET MAP C4

Sells books on – and by – leading Dutch artists and graphic designers, with a good sideline in entertaining postcards.

BRINKMAN

Singel 319 020 623 8353, antiquariaatbrinkman.nl. Mon–Fri 10am–5pm & Sat 11am–5pm. MAP PP.54–55, POCKET MAP A13

A stalwart of the Amsterdam antiquarian book trade, Brinkman has lots of good local stuff with expert advice if and when you need it.

'T CURIOSA WINKELTJE

Prinsengracht 228 020 625 1352. Mon 1–5.30pm, Tues–Fri 10am–5.30pm & Sat 10am–5pm. MAP PP.54–55, POCKET MAP C3

A jumble of bargain-basement glassware and crockery, candlesticks, antique tin toys, kitsch souvenirs, old apothecaries' jars and flasks. Perfect for browsing.

EDUARD KRAMER

Prinsengracht 807 020 626 1116, antique-tileshop.nl. Mon 11am–6pm, Tues–Sat 10am–6pm, Sun 1–6pm. MAP PP.54–55, POCKET MAP C6

Holds a wonderful selection of Dutch tiles from the fifteenth century onwards; it also operates an online ordering service.

EPISODE

Berenstraat 1 020 626 4679, episode.eu. Mon–Wed 11am–6pm, Thurs 11am–8pm, Fri 11am–7pm, Sat 10am–7pm, Sun noon–6pm. MAP PP.54–55, POCKET MAP C4

One of the larger secondhand stores, with everything from army jackets to hats, fur coats, shoes and belts. Specializes in the 1970s and 1980s.

GERDA'S BLOEMEN

Runstraat 16 020 624 2912, theninestreets.com. Mon–Fri 9am–6pm & Sat 9am–5pm. MAP PP.54–55 ,POCKET MAP C4

Amsterdam is full of flower shops, but this one is the most imaginative. Bouquets to melt the hardest of hearts.

DE KAASKAMER

Runstraat 7 020 623 3483, kaaskamer.nl. Mon noon–6pm, Tues–Fri 9am–6pm, Sat 9am–5pm & Sun noon–5pm. MAP PP.54–55, POCKET MAP C4

LAURA DOLS

PUCCINI BOMBONI

Friendly shop with a comprehensive selection of Dutch cheeses – much more than ordinary Edam – plus olives and international wines.

LAURA DOLS

Wolvenstraat 7 ⓣ 020 624 9066, ⓦ lauradols .nl. Mon–Sat 11am–6pm, Thurs until 7pm, Sun noon–6pm. MAP PP.54–55, POCKET MAP C4

Superb – and superbly creative – assortment of vintage clothing from dresses through to hats. Its forte is 1940s and 1950s gear.

MARLIES DEKKERS

Berenstraat 18 ⓣ 020 421 1900, ⓦ marliesdekkers.com. Mon 1-6pm, Tues-Sat 11am-6pm, Sun noon-5pm. MAP PP.54–55, POCKET MAP C4

One of Holland's most successful lingerie designers, Dekkers launched her first collection in 1993 to general acclaim from the fashion industry. Her range is sleek and stylish with a good dash of originality.

PUCCINI BONBONI

Singel 184, junction of Oude Leliestraat ⓣ 020 427 8341, ⓦ puccinibomboni.com. Mon noon–6pm, Tues–Sat 11am–6pm & Sun noon–6pm. MAP PP.54–55, POCKET MAP A11

Without doubt the best chocolatier in town, selling a wonderfully creative range of chocs in all sorts of shapes and sizes. This mini-chain has also abandoned the tweeness of the traditional chocolatier for brisk modern decor. There's another outlet in one of the quaintest parts of the city at Staalstraat 17 (see p.47).

WITTE TANDEN WINKEL

Runstraat 5 ⓣ 020 623 3443. ⓦ dewittetandenwinkel.nl. Tues–Sat 10am–5pm. MAP PP.54–55, POCKET MAP C4

The "White Teeth Shop" sells wacky toothbrushes and just about every dental hygiene accoutrement you can imagine.

Coffeeshops

THE BULLDOG

Leidseplein 15 ⓣ 020 422 3444. Thurs 10am–1am, Fri & Sat 10am–3am & Sun 10am–2am. MAP PP.54–55, POCKET MAP C5

The biggest and most famous of the coffeeshop chains, and a long way from its poky Red Light District origins. This, the main Leidseplein branch (the Palace), housed in a former police station, has a cocktail bar, coffeeshop, juice bar and souvenir shop. It's big and brash, not at all the place for a quiet smoke, though the dope they sell (packaged in neat little branded bags) is reliably good.

HAPPY FEELINGS

Kerkstraat 51 ⓣ 020 777 9898. Mon–Sat 9am–1am. MAP PP.54–55, POCKET MAP C5

What used to be a hippie hangout, turned into a fresh and trendy coffeeshop with flatscreens on the walls, attracting a select clientele.

SIBERIË

Brouwersgracht 11 T 020 623 6909. Daily 10am–11pm. MAP PP.54–55, POCKET MAP B10

Very relaxed, very friendly, this bright, modern coffeeshop is one of the city's most appealing, with magazines and a chessboard or two.

THE OTHERSIDE

Reguliersdwarsstraat 6 T 020 421 1014. Daily 11am–1am. MAP PP.54–55, POCKET MAP A14

Essentially a gay coffeeshop (in Dutch, "the other side" is a euphemism for gay), but straight-friendly and with a fun atmosphere.

Cafés and tearooms

BUFFET VAN ODETTE

Prinsengracht 598 T 020 423 6034, W buffet-amsterdam.nl. Daily 10am–10pm. MAP PP.54–55, POCKET MAP D6

Smart, modern and attractive café serving excellent light meals and salads, plus more substantial meals in the evening. The fresh pasta dishes are especially good (from €12).

GREENWOODS

Singel 103 T 020 623 7071, W greenwoods .eu. Mon–Thurs 9.30am–5pm, Fri–Sun 9.30am–6pm. MAP PP.54–55, POCKET MAP B11

Cosy English-style teashop in the basement of a canal house. Pies and sandwiches, pots of tea – and a decent breakfast.

PANINI

Vijzelgracht 3–5 T 020 626 4939, W restaurantpanini.nl. Mon–Sat 9am–11pm, Sun 11am–11pm. MAP PP.54–55, POCKET MAP D6

Formica may be a thing of the past almost everywhere else, but not here, giving this split-level Italian café a vaguely beatnik air. Great coffee, pasta and snacks during the day; reasonably priced meat, fish and pasta dishes at night.

DE BELHAMEL

Restaurants

BAR HUF

Reguliersdwarsstraat 43 T 020 303 9561, W barhuf.nl. Mon–Thurs & Sun 4pm–1am, Fri & Sat 4pm–3am. MAP PP.54–55, POCKET MAP A14

Perfect for late-night dining, *Bar Huf* has a straightforward gastropub menu – burgers, ribs and salads, etc – but the food is a cut above the average, fresh and tasty. Main courses start from €10.

DE BELHAMEL

Brouwersgracht 60 T 020 622 1095, W belhamel.nl. Daily noon–4pm & 6–10pm. MAP PP.54–55, POCKET MAP B10

Smashing restaurant where the Art Nouveau decor makes for a delightful setting and the menu is short but extremely well-chosen, mixing Dutch with French dishes. Main courses at around €20–25.

BOLHOED

Prinsengracht 60 T 020 626 1803. Daily noon–9.30pm. MAP PP.54–55, POCKET MAP C2

Something of an Amsterdam institution, the daily changing menu here features familiar vegan and vegetarian options, with organic beer to wash it down. Mains at around €15.

BRASSERIE AMBASSADE

Herengracht 339 ⓣ 020 555 0255, ⓦ brasserieambassade.nl. Daily 6–10pm. MAP P.P.54–55, POCKET MAP A13

Chic, modern restaurant in an old canal house – and a side-line for the excellent *Ambassade Hotel* (see p.127). An outstanding menu – try, for example, the lobster and beurre noisette. Mains average €20.

BUSSIA

Reestraat 28 ⓣ 020 627 8794, ⓦ bussia.nl. Tues 6–9.30pm, Wed–Sun noon–2pm & 6–9.30pm. MAP PP.54–55, POCKET MAP C3

Top-notch Italian restaurant with the freshest of ingredients. Everything is home-made, from the original Italian *gelato* to the pasta. Mains around €25, a bit less for pasta.

CAFÉ DE KLEPEL

Prinsenstraat 22 ⓣ 020 623 8244, ⓦ cafedeklepel.nl. Mon–Fri 6pm–midnight, Sat 4pm–midnight, Sun 4–10pm. MAP PP.54–55, POCKET MAP A10

Long-established brown bar turned into first-rate restaurant, an intimate sort of place serving up delicious French-inspired dishes from a short but finely tuned menu. Three-course set menu €35.

CHEZ GEORGES

Herenstraat 3 ⓣ 020 626 3332, ⓦ chez-georges.nl. Tues–Sun 6–11pm. MAP PP.54–55, POCKET MAP A11

This much-lauded French restaurant offers immaculately presented dishes, with main course €23 and up. The old fashioned interior adds to the homely feel. Has an excellent selection of wines, too.

D'ANTICA

Reguliersdwarsstraat 80 ⓣ 020 623 3862, ⓦ dantica.nl. Mon–Thurs 7–10pm, Fri & Sat 7–11pm. MAP PP.54–55, POCKET MAP B14

Slick and modern Italian restaurant serving authentic cuisine, including a particularly tasty risotto with wild mushrooms and pork sausage. In the heart of the urban action, near Rembrandtplein. Main courses average €25.

FYRA

Noorderstraat 19–23 ⓣ 020 428 3632, ⓦ restaurantfyra.nl. Daily 6pm–midnight. MAP PP.54–55, POCKET MAP D6

Smart, modern restaurant with a wide-ranging international menu that focuses on local, seasonal ingredients – try, for example, the lamb with apricots. They have an excellent wine list too. Three-course menu €36.

GOLDEN TEMPLE

Utrechtsestraat 126 ⓣ 020 626 8560, ⓦ restaurantgoldentemple.com. Daily 5–9.30pm. MAP PP.54–55, POCKET MAP E6

Laidback place with a little more soul than the average Amsterdam veggie joint. Pleasant, attentive service. No alcohol.

PANCAKE BAKERY

PANCAKE BAKERY

Prinsengracht 191 ⓣ 020 625 1333, ⓦ pancake.nl. Daily 9am–9.30pm. MAP PP.54–55, POCKET MAP C2

Located in the basement of an old canal house, this restaurant offers a mind-boggling range of fillings for its pancakes (€8–14). A tourist favourite.

PREGO

Herenstraat 25 ⓣ 020 638 0148, ⓦ restaurantprego.nl. Mon–Fri 6–10pm, Sat & Sun 12.30–3pm & 6–10pm. MAP PP.54–55, POCKET MAP A11

Informal French-Mediterranean restaurant with modern decor offering tasty dishes such *coq au vin, bouillabaisse* and red sea bass with couscous. Mains average €25.

PURI MAS

Lange Leidsedwarsstraat 37 ⓣ 020 627 7627, ⓦ purimas.nl. Daily 5–11pm. MAP PP.54–55, POCKET MAP C5

Exceptionally good value Indonesian, on a street better known for rip-offs. Friendly and informed service preludes spectacular *rijsttafels*, both meat and vegetarian.

SHIVA

Reguliersdwarsstraat 72 ⓣ 020 624 8713, ⓦ shivarestaurant.nl. Daily 5–11pm. MAP PP.54–55, POCKET MAP B14

Competent Indian restaurant with a wide selection of dishes, all well prepared and moderately priced.

STOUT

Haarlemmerstraat 73 ⓣ 020 616 3664, ⓦ restaurantstout.nl. Daily 10am–1am, Sun from 11am. MAP PP.54–55, POCKET MAP B10

Lively and fashionable café-restaurant, popular with locals. Great sandwiches and salads at daytime and everything from duck to fresh oysters in the evening.

STOUT

TASTE OF VIETNAM

Herenstraat 28 ⓣ 020 358 6715, ⓦ thetasteofvietnam.nl. Tues–Sun 4.30–10.30pm. MAP PP.54–55, POCKET MAP A11

One of the best Vietnamese restaurants in Amsterdam, a briskly decorated modern place offering the tastiest of spring rolls, soups and noodle dishes. You can also order a chef's tasting menu. Mains from €14.

TEMPO DOELOE

Utrechtsestraat 75 ⓣ 020 625 6718, ⓦ tempodoeloerestaurant.nl. Mon–Sat 6–11pm. MAP PP.54–55, POCKET MAP E6

Small and smart Indonesian restaurant with authentic cuisine and attentive service. It's a popular spot, so reservations are strongly advised. Mains from €15.

VAN DE KAART

Prinsengracht 512 ⓣ 020 625 9232, ⓦ vandekaart.com. Mon–Sat 5.30–10.30pm. MAP PP.54–55, POCKET MAP C6

Slick restaurant, with an enterprising French-inspired menu including poached lobster, smoked mackerel and beef cheek stew-stuffed ravioli. Excellent wine list.

Bars

ARENDSNEST

Herengracht 90 ⓣ 020 421 2057, ⓦ arendsnest.nl. Daily noon–midnight. MAP PP.54–55, POCKET MAP A11

In a handsome old canal house, this bar boasts impressive wooden decor – from the longest of bars to the tall wood-and-glass cabinets – and specializes in Dutch beers, of which it has over 100 varieties.

LA CAGE

Regulierdwarsstraat 44 ⓣ 020 320 9108, ⓦ lacageamsterdam.nl. Tues–Sun 4pm–1am, Fri & Sat until 3am. MAP PP.54–55, POCKET MAP B14

Huge, fashionable and gay-friendly, with slick decor and multiple bars. Cocktail nights and DJs at weekends.

OOSTERLING

Utrechtsestraat 140 ⓣ 020 623 4140, ⓦ cafeoosterling.nl. Mon–Wed 3–11.30pm, Thurs–Sat noon–1am & Sun 1–8pm. MAP PP.54–55, POCKET MAP E6

Stone-floored, neighbourhood bar-cum-off-licence that's long been owned by the same family. Specializes in *jenever* (gin), with dozens of brands and varieties.

HET PAPENEILAND

Prinsengracht 2 ⓣ 020 624 1989, ⓦ papeneiland.nl. Daily 10am–1am. MAP PP.54–55, POCKET MAP C1

With its wood panelling, antique Delft tiles and ancient stove, this is one of the cosiest bars in the Grachtengordel. It gets packed late at night with a garrulous crew.

DE PIEPER

Prinsengracht 424 ⓣ 020 626 4775. Mon–Sat noon–1am, Sun 2–8pm. MAP PP.54–55, POCKET MAP C5

Relaxed neighbourhood brown bar with rickety old furniture and a terrace beside the canal.

DE PRINS

Prinsengracht 124 ⓣ 020 624 9382, ⓦ deprins.nl. Daily 10am–1am. MAP PP.54–55, POCKET MAP C2

This popular and lively brown bar has well-worn decor, live bands and a chatty atmosphere. Also offers a wide range of drinks and well-priced food, served 10am–10pm.

SPANJER & VAN TWIST

Leliegracht 60 ⓣ 020 639 0109, ⓦ spanjerenvantwist.nl. Daily 10am–1am. MAP PP.54–55, POCKET MAP C2

Hip café-bar with an arty air and modern fittings. Tasty snacks and light meals plus an outside mini-terrace right on the canal.

VIVE LA VIE

Amstelstraat 7 ⓣ 020 624 0114, ⓦ vivelavie .net. Daily 4pm–3am, Fri & Sat until 4am. MAP PP.54–55, POCKET MAP C14

Small bar, patronized mostly, but not exclusively, by women and transvestites. Quiet during the week, it steams on the weekend.

SPANJER & VAN TWIST

THE WATERHOLE

Korte Leidsedwarsstraat 49 ⓣ 020 620 8904, ⓦ waterhole.nl. Mon–Thurs & Sun 2pm–3am, Fri & Sat 2pm–4am. MAP PP.54–55, POCKET MAP C5

Late-night bar with live music most nights, anything from punk and rock to jazz and blues. It's especially popular for its regular Monday "new bands" sessions, which attract a raucous but friendly crew; cheap beer too.

WEBER

Marnixstraat 397 ⓣ 020 622 9910, ⓦ weberlux.nl. Daily 7pm–3am, Fri & Sat until 4am. MAP PP.54–55, POCKET MAP B5

Popular local hangout attracting musicians, students and young professionals. Crowded at weekends but friendly.

Clubs and venues

ESCAPE

Rembrandtplein 11 ⓣ 020 622 1111, ⓦ escape.nl. Thurs–Sun 11pm–4/5am. MAP PP.54–55, POCKET MAP C14

This vast club has space enough for 2 people. It once hosted Amsterdam's cutting edge Chemistry nights and has an ear-bashing soundsystem that appeals to mainstream punters.

JAZZ CAFÉ ALTO

Korte Leidsedwarsstraat 115 ⓣ 020 626 3249, ⓦ jazz-cafe-alto.com. Daily 9pm–3am. MAP PP.54–55, POCKET MAP C5

It's worth hunting down this legendary little jazz bar just off Leidseplein for its quality modern jazz. It's big on atmosphere, though slightly cramped, and entry is free.

JIMMY WOO

Korte Leidsedwarsstraat 18 ⓣ 020 626 3150, ⓦ www.jimmywoo.com. Wed–Sun 11pm–3/4am. MAP PP.54–55, POCKET MAP C5

Intimate and stylish club spread over two floors. Upstairs, the black lacquered walls, Japanese lamps and cosy booths with leather couches ooze sexy chic, while downstairs a packed dance floor throbs under hundreds of oscillating lightbulbs studded into the ceiling. Popular with young, well-dressed locals so look smart if you want to join in.

MELKWEG (MILKY WAY)

Lijnbaansgracht 234a ⓣ 020 531 8181, ⓦ melkweg.nl. Opening hours vary, see website. MAP PP.54–55, POCKET MAP B5

Probably Amsterdam's most famous entertainment venue. A former dairy (hence the name) just round the corner from Leidseplein, this has two

JIMMY WOO

MELKWEG (MILKY WAY)

separate halls for live music, and puts on a broad range of bands covering everything from reggae to rock, all of which lean towards the "alternative". Excellent DJ sessions go on late at the weekend. There's also a monthly film programme, a theatre, gallery and café-restaurant (Marnixstraat entrance).

PARADISO

Weteringschans 6–8 ⓣ 020 626 4521, ⓦ paradiso.nl. MAP PP.54–55, POCKET MAP C6

A converted church near the Leidseplein, revered by many for its excellent programme, featuring local and international bands. Club nights draw in the crowds, and look out also for DJ sets on Fridays and Saturdays. Sometimes hosts classical concerts, as well as debates and multimedia events.

STADSSCHOUWBURG

Leidseplein 26 ⓣ 020 624 2311, ⓦ stadsschouwburgamsterdam.nl. MAP PP.54–55, POCKET MAP B5

Long-established concert hall in the thick of Amsterdam's nightlife offering a wide range of performances, including theatre, opera and dance by both Dutch and foreign troupes.

STUDIO 80

Rembrandtplein 17 ⓣ 020 521 8333, ⓦ www.studio-80.nl. Wed–Sat from 10pm. MAP PP.54–55, POCKET MAP C14

Right on the Rembrandtplein, this place celebrates the underground scene with techno, soul, funk, minimal and electro. A breeding ground for upcoming DJs and bands.

SUGAR FACTORY

Lijnbaansgracht 238 ⓣ 020 627 8, ⓦ sugarfactory.nl. Daily 6pm–5am. MAP PP.54–55, POCKET MAP C5

Opposite the *Melkweg*, *Sugar Factory* pulls in a young, trendy crowd and has an underground vibe. Regular nights include Techno Tuesday, Wednesday's "Night Shift" (hip-hop, disco and house) and Sunday's "Wicked Jazz", with DJs and musicians putting on a mix of jazz, r'n'b and funk.

THEATER CARRÉ

Amstel 115–125 ⓣ 0900 2525 255, ⓦ carre.nl. MAP PP.54–55, POCKET MAP F6

A splendid late-nineteenth-century structure comprises the ultimate venue for Dutch folk artists, and hosts all kinds of top international acts – anything from Van Morrison to Carmen, with reputable touring orchestras and opera companies squeezed in between.

The Jordaan and western docklands

On the western side of the city centre, the Jordaan is an area of slender canals and narrow streets flanked by an agreeable mix of modest, modern terraces and handsome seventeenth-century canal houses. It was traditionally the home of Amsterdam's working class, but in recent decades it has become one of the most sought-after residential neighbourhoods in the city. Until the 1970s, the inhabitants were primarily stevedores and factory workers earning a crust in the Scheepvaartsbuurt (Shipping Quarter) that edges the north of the Jordaan. This quarter is now a mixed shopping and residential area, while just beyond, the Westerdok is the oldest part of the sprawling complex of artificial islands that sweeps along both sides of the River IJ.

THE JORDAAN

MAP P.73, POCKET MAP B3

According to dyed-in-the-wool locals, the true Jordaaner is born within earshot of the Westerkerk bells, which means that there are endless arguments as to quite where the district's southern boundary lies, though at least the other borders are clear – Prinsengracht, Brouwersgracht and Lijnbaansgracht. The streets just north of Leidsegracht – often deemed to be the southern border – are routinely modern, though **Looiersgracht**, running either side of its canal, does have its scenic moments.

ELANDSGRACHT

MAP P.73, POCKET MAP B4

The narrow streets and canals just to the north of the Looiersgracht are pleasant if unremarkable, but **Elandsgracht** does hold, at no. 109, the enjoyable indoor antiques centre **Antiekcentrum Amsterdam** (see p.76). Football fanatics will also want to take a peek at the Smit-Cruyff sports shop at Elandsgracht 98, where the recently deceased **Johan Cruyff** – star of Ajax in the

ANTIEKCENTRUM AMSTERDAM

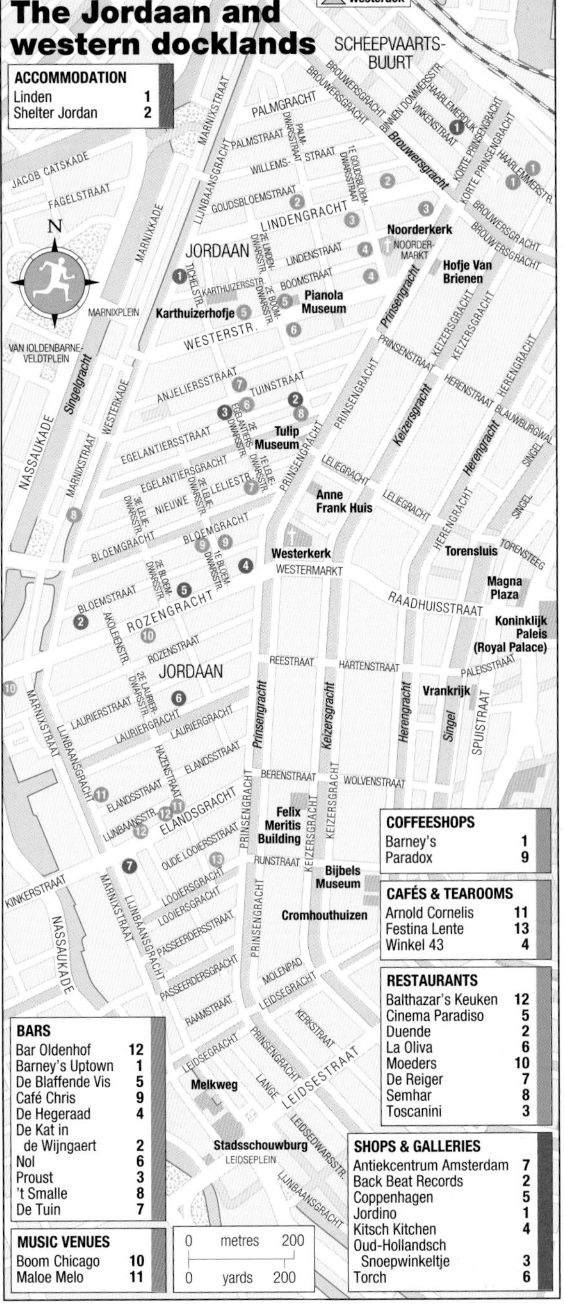
The Jordaan and western docklands
ACCOMMODATION
Linden 1
Shelter Jordan 2
COFFEESHOPS
Barney's 1
Paradox 9
CAFÉS & TEAROOMS
Arnold Cornelis 11
Festina Lente 13
Winkel 43 4
RESTAURANTS
Balthazar's Keuken 12
Cinema Paradiso 5
Duende 2
La Oliva 6
Moeders 10
De Reiger 7
Semhar 8
Toscanini 3
BARS
Bar Oldenhof 12
Barney's Uptown 1
De Blaffende Vis 5
Café Chris 9
De Hegeraad 4
De Kat in de Wijngaert 2
Nol 6
Proust 3
't Smalle 8
De Tuin 7
MUSIC VENUES
Boom Chicago 10
Maloe Melo 11
SHOPS & GALLERIES
Antiekcentrum Amsterdam 7
Back Beat Records 2
Coppenhagen 5
Jordino 1
Kitsch Kitchen 4
Oud-Hollandsch Snoepwinkeltje 3
Torch 6
0 metres 200
0 yards 200
Westerdok
SCHEEPVAARTS-BUURT
JORDAAN
Noorderkerk
NOORDERMARKT
Hofje Van Brienen
Pianola Museum
Karthuizerhofje
Tulip Museum
Anne Frank Huis
Westerkerk
WESTERMARKT
Torensluis
Magna Plaza
Koninklijk Paleis (Royal Palace)
Vrankrijk
Felix Meritis Building
Bijbels Museum
Cromhouthuizen
Melkweg
Stadsschouwburg
LEIDSEPLEIN
MARNIXPLEIN
VAN IOLDENBARNEVELDTPLEIN
JACOB CATSKADE
FAGELSTRAAT
MARNIXKADE
MARNIXSTRAAT
LIJNBAANSGRACHT
Singelgracht
NASSAUKADE
WESTERKADE
PALMGRACHT
PALMSTRAAT
WILLEMSSTRAAT
GOUDSBLOEMSTRAAT
LINDENGRACHT
LINDENSTRAAT
BOOMSTRAAT
KARTHUIZERSSTR.
TICHELSTR.
WESTERSTR.
ANJELIERSSTRAAT
TUINSTRAAT
EGELANTIERSSTRAAT
EGELANTIERSGRACHT
NIEUWE LELIESTR.
BLOEMGRACHT
BLOEMSTRAAT
ROZENGRACHT
ROZENSTRAAT
AKOLEIENSTR.
LAURIERSTRAAT
LAURIERGRACHT
HAZENSTRAAT
ELANDSSTRAAT
ELANDSGRACHT
OUDE LOOIERSSTRAAT
LOOIERSGRACHT
PASSEERDERSSTRAAT
PASSEERDERSGRACHT
RAAMSTRAAT
KINKERSTRAAT
LEIDSEGRACHT
LANGE LEIDSEDWARSSTR.
LEIDSESTRAAT
KERKSTRAAT
MOLENPAD
RUNSTRAAT
BERENSTRAAT
WOLVENSTRAAT
REESTRAAT
HARTENSTRAAT
RAADHUISSTRAAT
PALEISSTRAAT
SPUISTRAAT
Singel
Herengracht
Keizersgracht
Prinsengracht
PRINSENGRACHT
KEIZERSGRACHT
HERENGRACHT
LELIEGRACHT
PRINSENSTRAAT
HERENSTRAAT
BLAUWBURGWAL
TORENSTEEG
BROUWERSGRACHT
Brouwersgracht
BINNEN DOMMERSSTR.
HAARLEMERDIJK
VINKENSTRAAT
KORTE PRINSENGRACHT
HAARLEMMERSTR.

1970s and one of the greatest players of all time – bought his first pair of football boots. Nearby, at the east end of Elandsgracht you might pause to look at the **statues** of **Johnny Jordaan** (1924–89) and **Tante Leen** (1912–92) – two singers who were for years the sound of the working-class Jordaan, and whose songs are still remembered and sung in some of the area's more raucous cafés.

ROZENGRACHT

MAP P.73, POCKET MAP B3

A few blocks further north, the area's main artery, **Rozengracht**, slices through the centre of the Jordaan, though this wide street lost most of its character when its canal was filled in and is now a busy main road. It was here, at no. 184, that Rembrandt spent the last ten years of his life in diminished circumstances – a plaque distinguishes his old home.

BLOEMGRACHT

MAP P.73, POCKET MAP B3

The streets and canals between Rozengracht and Westerstraat form the heart of the Jordaan and hold the district's prettiest sights. North of Rozengracht, the first canal is the **Bloemgracht** (Flower Canal), a leafy waterway dotted with houseboats and arched by dinky little bridges, its network of cross-streets sprinkled with cafés, bars and idiosyncratic shops. There's a warm, relaxed community atmosphere here which is really rather beguiling, not to mention a clutch of fine old canal houses. Pride of architectural place goes to **Bloemgracht 87–91**, a sterling Renaissance building of 1642 complete with a trio of distinctive facade stones, representing a *steeman* (city-dweller), a *landman* (farmer) and a *seeman* (sailor). **Nos. 83–85** next door were built a few decades later.

TULIP MUSEUM

Prinsengracht 116, at Egelantiersgracht ⓣ 020 421 0095, ⓦ amsterdamtulipmuseum.com. Daily 10am–6pm. €5. MAP P.73, POCKET MAP C2

More of a shop than a museum, the **Tulip Museum** sells all sorts of flower-related items upstairs, while down below is a moderately interesting exhibition on the history of the tulip with some details on the speculative bubble in tulip prices that ripped through the Netherlands in the Golden Age.

BLOEMGRACHT

PIANOLA MUSEUM

Westerstraat 106 ⓣ 020 627 9624, ⓦ pianola .nl. Sun 2–5pm. €5. MAP P.73, POCKET MAP C2

Busy Westerstraat is fairly ordinary, but it's here you'll find the small but charming **Pianola Museum**, which has a collection of **pianolas** and automatic music machines dating from the beginning of the twentieth century, fifteen of which have been restored to working order. These machines were the jukeboxes of their day, and the museum has a vast collection of over fifteen thousand rolls of music, some of which were "recorded" by famous pianists and composers – Gershwin, Debussy, Scott Joplin and others. It also runs a regular programme of pianola music concerts (check their website).

KARTHUIZERHOFJE

Karthuizersstraat 89–171. Daily 10am–8pm. Free. MAP P.73, POCKET MAP B2

Tucked away behind a white doorway, the seventeenth-century **Karthuizerhofje** is the largest of Jordaan's **hofjes** (alms houses). The substantial courtyard complex has picket-fenced gardens and old ornate water-pumps, and makes a peaceful port of call.

LINDENGRACHT

MAP P.73, POCKET MAP C1

Lindengracht (Canal of Limes) lost its waterway decades ago, and is now a quiet and fairly nondescript thoroughfare flanked for the most part by an indeterminate mix of twentieth-century apartment blocks. The east end of Lindengracht intersects with **Brouwersgracht** (see p.52), one of Amsterdam's prettiest streets.

THE SCHEEPVAARTSBUURT AND THE WESTERDOK

MAP P.73, POCKET MAP C1

Brouwersgracht marks both the northern edge of the Jordaan and the southern boundary of the **Scheepvaartsbuurt** – the Shipping Quarter. In the eighteenth and nineteenth centuries, this district boomed from its location between the Brouwersgracht and the **Westerdok**, a parcel of land dredged out of the River IJ immediately to the north and equipped with docks, warehouses and shipyards. The Westerdok hung on to some of the marine trade until the 1960s, but today the area is busy reinventing itself, as the old warehouses are turned into apartments. The **Westerpark** provides a spot of green for the locals, and the **Westergasfabriek** (ⓦ westergasfabriek.nl), a former gasworks, has been turned into a cultural zone full of design companies and restaurants; it hosts a fashion market on the first Sunday of each month. A short walk away, under the rail tracks and left down Zaanstraat, the 1921 **Het Schip** housing development is a seminal work of the Amsterdam School and can be visited on hourly tours (ⓦ hetschip.nl, Tues–Sun 11am–5pm; €12.50).

Shops

ANTIEKCENTRUM AMSTERDAM

Elandsgracht 109 ⓣ 020 624 9038, ⓦ antiekcentrumamsterdam.nl. Mon & Wed–Fri 11am–6pm, Sat & Sun 11am–5pm. MAP P.73, POCKET MAP B4

This indoor antiques centre is the city's largest with over fifty dealers offering an enormous choice, from vintage watches and jewellery to 1960s ceramics.

BACK BEAT RECORDS

Egelantiersstraat 19 ⓣ 020 627 1657, ⓦ backbeat.nl. Mon–Sat 11am–6pm. MAP P.73, POCKET MAP C2

Small specialist in soul, blues, jazz and funk, with a helpful and enthusiastic owner. New and secondhand vinyl and CDs.

COPPENHAGEN

Rozengracht 54 ⓣ 020 624 3681, ⓦ coppenhagenbeads.nl. Mon 1–6pm, Tues–Fri 10am–6pm, Sat 10am–5pm. MAP P.73, POCKET MAP B3

This Jordaan institution stocks beads and beady accessories – including everything you'll need to make your own jewellery.

JORDINO

Haarlemmerdijk 25a ⓣ 020 420 3225, ⓦ jordino.nl. Sun & Mon 1–6.30pm, Tues–Sat 10am–6.30pm. MAP P.73, POCKET MAP D1

BARNEY'S

Super handmade chocolates and arguably the city's best ice cream.

KITSCH KITCHEN

Rozengracht 8 ⓣ 020 462 0050, ⓦ kitschkitchen.nl. Mon–Sat 10am–6pm, Sun noon–5pm. MAP P.73, POCKET MAP C3

Crammed full of substantial furniture and brightly coloured home and kitchen stuff – you're bound to find something you think you need here.

OUD-HOLLANDSCH SNOEPWINKELTJE

Tweede Egelantierdwarsstraat 2 ⓣ 020 420 7390, ⓦ snoepwinkeltje.com. Tues–Sat 11am–6.30pm, Sun noon-5pm. MAP P.73, POCKET MAP C2

Delicious Dutch sweets, piled up in glass jars attracting hordes of kids.

TORCH

Lauriergracht 94 ⓣ 020 626 0284, ⓦ torchgallery.com. Thurs–Sat noon–6pm. MAP P.73, POCKET MAP B4

Established in 1984, this is one of the city's most adventurous, sometimes obscurantist, contemporary art galleries.

Coffeeshops

BARNEY'S

Haarlemmerstraat 102 ⓣ 020 625 7390. Daily 8am–1am. MAP P.73, POCKET MAP D1

This popular coffeeshop is one of the most civilized places in town to enjoy a big hit before moving on to *Barney's Uptown* just along the road for a drink.

PARADOX

1e Bloemdwarsstraat 2 ⓣ 020 623 5639. Daily 10am–8pm. MAP P.73, POCKET MAP B3

Paradox satisfies the munchies with outstanding natural food, including spectacular fresh fruit concoctions and veggie burgers.

Cafés and tearooms

ARNOLD CORNELIS

Elandsgracht 78 ⓣ 020 625 8585, ⓦ cornelis.nl. Mon–Fri 8.30am–6pm, Sat 8.30am–5pm. MAP P.73, POCKET MAP B4

Confectioner and patisserie with a mouthwatering display of pastries and cakes. Take away or eat in the snug tearoom.

FESTINA LENTE

Looiersgracht 40b ⓣ 020 638 1412, ⓦ cafefestinalente.nl. Mon–Thurs noon–1am, Fri noon–3am, Sat 10.30am–3am, Sun noon–1am. MAP P.73, POCKET MAP B4

Relaxed neighbourhood café-bar with armchairs. The outside tables overlooking the canal are a suntrap in summer.

WINKEL 43

Noordermarkt 43 ⓣ 020 623 0223, ⓦ winkel43.nl. Mon 7am–1am, Tues–Thurs 8am–1am, Fri 8am–3am, Sat 7am–3am, Sun 10am–1am. MAP P.73, POCKET MAP C2

Queue up along with the rest of Amsterdam for delectable mouthwatering apple pie –it's home-made in this popular lunchroom-cum-restaurant.

Restaurants

BALTHAZAR'S KEUKEN

Elandsgracht 108 ⓣ 020 420 2114, ⓦ balthazarskeuken.nl. Wed–Sat 6–10.30pm. MAP P.73, POCKET MAP B4

As the name suggests, you feel like you accidentally stumbled into someone's kitchen here. Their weekly changing three-course menu (€40) is very popular. Be sure to book.

CINEMA PARADISO

Westerstraat 186 ⓣ 020 623 7344, ⓦ cinemaparadiso.info. Tues–Sun 6–11pm. MAP P.73, POCKET MAP C2

Slick place covering all the Italian classics with gusto. It's in a former moviehouse and very popular. Pasta, pizzas from €16.

DUENDE

Lindengracht 62 ⓣ 020 420 6692, ⓦ cafe-duende.nl. Mon–Fri 4pm–midnight, Sat noon–1am, Sun 2pm–midnight. Kitchen until 10.30pm. MAP P.73, POCKET MAP C1

Busy tapas bar with a tiled interior and a warm and inviting feel. Good food, and there's also a small venue that hosts flamenco at weekends.

LA OLIVA

Egelantiersstraat 122 ⓣ 020 320 4316, ⓦ la-oliva.nl. Daily noon–10pm. MAP P.73, POCKET MAP C2

Specializes in *pinxtos*, the delectable Basque snacks-on-sticks that make Spanish bar-hopping such a delight.

MOEDERS

Rozengracht 251 ⓣ 020 626 7957, ⓦ moeders.com. Mon–Fri 5pm–midnight, Sat & Sun noon–midnight; kitchen till 10.30pm. MAP P.73, POCKET MAP B3

Really cosy restaurant just across from the Singelgracht whose theme is obvious the moment you walk in – mothers, photos of whom plaster the walls. Food is engagingly homespun Dutch grub with the odd modern twist, very tasty and reasonably priced.

WINKEL 43

DE REIGER

Nieuwe Leliestraat 34 020 624 7426, dereigeramsterdam.nl. Tues–Fri 5–10.30pm, Sat noon–4pm & 6–10.30pm, Sun 4–10.30pm. MAP P.73, POCKET MAP C3

In the thick of the Jordaan, this is an old-style brown café filled with modish Amsterdammers. Mains around €25.

SEMHAR

Marnixstraat 259–261 020 638 1634, semhar.nl. Tues–Sun 4–10pm. MAP P.73, POCKET MAP B3

A small and popular Ethiopian restaurant with an authentic menu of meat, fish and veggie dishes (mains around €15) – all mopped up with a large and spongy flatbread. Try the African beer too, which comes served in a *calabash*.

TOSCANINI

Lindengracht 75 020 623 2813, restauranttoscanini.nl. Mon–Sat 6pm–1.30am, kitchen till 10.30pm. MAP P.73, POCKET MAP C1

Big, bustling and authentic Italian restaurant, with great daily specials and an extensive regional Italian wine list.

TOSCANINI

Bars

BAR OLDENHOF

Elandsgracht 84 020 751 3273, bar-oldenhof.com. Daily 6pm–1am. MAP P.73, POCKET MAP B4

Lovely old-fashioned bar with opulent armchairs. Does a tip-top line in cocktails and single malt whisky; also has an excellent range of wines.

BARNEY'S UPTOWN

Haarlemmerstraat 105 020 427 9469, barneys.biz. Daily 8am–1am, Fri & Sat until 3am. MAP P.73, POCKET MAP D1

Pleasant, smoker-friendly bar that's the slick night-time sister of the coffeeshop along the street (see p.76), with DJs providing a humming backdrop. The American(ish) menu has a choice of burgers, steaks and sandwiches, plus huge breakfasts and weekend brunch.

DE BLAFFENDE VIS

Westerstraat 118 020 625 1721. Daily 9am–1am, Fri & Sat until 3am. MAP P.73, POCKET MAP C2

Something of an institution, this typical neighbourhood bar sits at the corner of the 2e Boomdwarsstraat. Oodles of atmosphere and a well-priced bar menu.

CAFÉ CHRIS

Bloemstraat 42 020 624 5942, cafechris.nl. Mon–Thurs 3pm–1am, Fri & Sat 3pm–2am, Sun 3–9pm. MAP P.73, POCKET MAP B3

This place is very proud of itself for being the Jordaan's (and Amsterdam's) oldest bar –it dates from 1624. The atmosphere is homely and cozy.

DE HEGERAAD

Noordermarkt 34 020 624 5565. Mon–Sat 8am–midnight, Sun 11am–11pm. MAP P.73, POCKET MAP C2

Lovingly maintained brown café with a loyal clientele. The back room is the perfect place to relax with a hot chocolate.

DE KAT IN DE WIJNGAERT

Lindengracht 160 020 622 4554, dekatindewijngaert.nl. Sun–Thurs 10am–1am, Fri 10am–3am, Sat 9am–3am MAP P.73, POCKET MAP C1

With the enticing name "The Cat in the Vineyard", this small bar is the epitome of the Jordaan local – and quiet enough for conversation.

NOL

Westerstraat 109. 020 624 5360, cafenol-amsterdam.nl. Wed, Thurs & Sun 9pm–3am, Fri & Sat 9pm–4am. MAP P.73, POCKET MAP C2

Raucous and jolly Jordaan singing bar. This luridly lit dive closes late, especially at weekends, when the back-slapping joviality and drunken sing-alongs keep you rooted until the small hours.

PROUST

Noordermarkt 4. Sun & Mon 9am–1am, Tues–Thurs noon–1am, Fri noon–3am, Sat 9am–3am. MAP P.73, POCKET MAP A10

Trendy bar (check out the giant "gun" chandelier) with a laidback Jordaan atmosphere, attracting students and young urban professionals. Reasonably priced bar menu (fish and chips €13) and drinks.

'T SMALLE

Egelantiersgracht 12 020 623 9617, t-smalle.nl. Daily 10am–1am. MAP P.73, POCKET MAP C2

Candlelit and comfortable, this is one of Amsterdam's oldest cafés: it opened in 1786 as a tasting house for the (long-gone) gin distillery next door. Its pontoon terrace is a perfect spot in summer – arrive early to nab a table.

DE TUIN

DE TUIN

2e Tuindwarsstraat 13 020 624 4559, cafedetuin.nl. Mon–Thurs 10am–1am, Fri & Sat 10am–3am, Sun 11am–1am. MAP P.73, POCKET MAP C2

The Jordaan has some marvellously unpretentious bars, and this is one of the best: unkempt and filled with locals.

Live music and venues

BOOM CHICAGO

Rozengracht 117 020 217 0400, www.boomchicago.nl. MAP P.73, POCKET MAP B3

This rapid-fire US improv comedy troupe performs nightly at the Rozentheater to crowds of tourists and locals.

MALOE MELO

Lijnbaansgracht 163 020 420 4592, www.maloemelo.com. Daily 9am–3am. MAP P.73, POCKET MAP B4

Dark, low-ceilinged bar, with a small back room featuring local blues acts. Jam sessions take place Sunday to Thursday.

The Old Jewish Quarter and Plantage

The narrow slice of land between the curve of the River Amstel, Oudeschans and the Nieuwe Herengracht was the home of Amsterdam's Jews from the sixteenth century up until World War II. By the 1920s, this Old Jewish Quarter, or Jodenhoek ("Jews' Corner"), was crowded with tenement buildings and smoking factories, its main streets holding scores of open-air stalls selling everything from pickled herrings to pots and pans. The war put paid to all this. In 1945 it lay derelict, and neither has postwar redevelopment treated it kindly; new building has robbed the district of much of its character. But persevere: amid the cars and concrete around Waterlooplein and Mr Visserplein are several moving reminders of the Jewish community that perished in the war, while the neighbouring residential area of Plantage is home to the Artis Zoo and the excellent Verzetsmuseum (Dutch Resistance Museum).

OUDESCHANS

Metro Nieuwmarkt. MAP PP.82–83, POCKET MAP D13

Wide and windy, the **Oudeschans** canal began life as Amsterdam's eastern moat until its original function was usurped when more land was dredged out of the River IJ. Thereafter, the Oudeschans was

THE REMBRANDTHUIS

home to a string of shipyards and, although these are long gone, the canal's defensive origins are still recalled by the Montelbaanstoren, a sturdy and conspicuous brick tower built in 1516. The tower's decorative spire was added later, when the city felt more secure, to a design by Hendrick de Keyser (1565–1621), the architect who did much to create Amsterdam's prickly skyline.

REMBRANDTHUIS

Jodenbreestraat 4 ⓣ 020 520 0400, ⓦ rembrandthuis.nl. Daily 10am–6pm. €13. MAP PP.82–83, POCKET MAP D13

Once the centre of Jewish life, Jodenbreestraat, the "Broad Street of the Jews", is short on charm, but it is home to the **Rembrandthuis**, whose intricate facade is decorated with pretty wooden shutters. Rembrandt bought this house at the height of his fame and popularity, living here for over twenty years and spending a fortune on furnishings – an expense that ultimately contributed to his bankruptcy. An inventory made at the time details the huge collection of paintings, sculptures and art treasures he'd amassed, almost all of which was auctioned off after he was declared insolvent and forced to move to a more modest house in the Jordaan in 1658.

The city council bought the Jodenbreestraat house in 1907 and has revamped the premises on several occasions, most recently in 1999. A visit begins in the modern building next door, but you're soon into the string of period rooms that have been returned to something like their appearance when Rembrandt lived here, with the original inventory as a guide. The period furniture is enjoyable enough, especially the box-beds, and the great man's studio is surprisingly large and well-lit, but it's the collection of seventeenth-century Dutch paintings that grabs most of the attention, notably several works by Rembrandt's master in Amsterdam, Pieter Lastman. On the same floor, in the **Salon**, is the museum's one and only Rembrandt, his *Portrait of the Preacher Eleazer Swalmius*, an early work currently on long-term loan from Antwerp. Beyond is the intriguing "Art Cabinet", a room crammed with objets d'art and miscellaneous curios including African spears and Pacific seashells. Beyond the Art Cabinet, the rest of the Rembrandthuis is usually given over to temporary exhibitions on the artist and his contemporaries. There's also, space permitting, a substantial assortment of Rembrandt's **etchings**, as well as several of the original copper plates on which he worked.

GASSAN DIAMONDS

Nieuwe Uilenburgerstraat 173 ⓣ 020 622 5333, ⓦ gassan.com. Frequent 30min guided tours daily 9am–5pm. Free; no advance booking required. MAP PP.82–83, POCKET MAP D13

Gassan Diamonds occupies a large and imposing brick building dating from 1897. Before World War II, many local Jews worked as diamond cutters and polishers, but there's little sign of the industry hereabouts today, this factory being the main exception. Tours include a visit to the cutting and polishing areas, as well a gambol round Gassan's diamond jewellery showroom.

STOPERA – STADHUIS & MUZIEKTHEATER

Muziektheater box office ⓣ 020 625 5455, ⓦ operaballet.nl. MAP PP.82–83, POCKET MAP D14

Jodenbreestraat runs parallel to the **Stadhuis en Muziektheater**, a sprawling and distinctly underwhelming modern complex dating from the 1980s and incorporating the city hall and a large auditorium. The Muziektheater offers a varied programme of theatre, dance and ballet as well as opera from the country's first-rate Netherlands Opera (De Nederlandse Opera; ⓦ operaballet.nl), but tickets go very quickly. One of the city's abiding ironies is that the title of the protest campaign aiming to prevent the development in the 1980s – "Stopera" – has passed into common usage to describe the finished item.

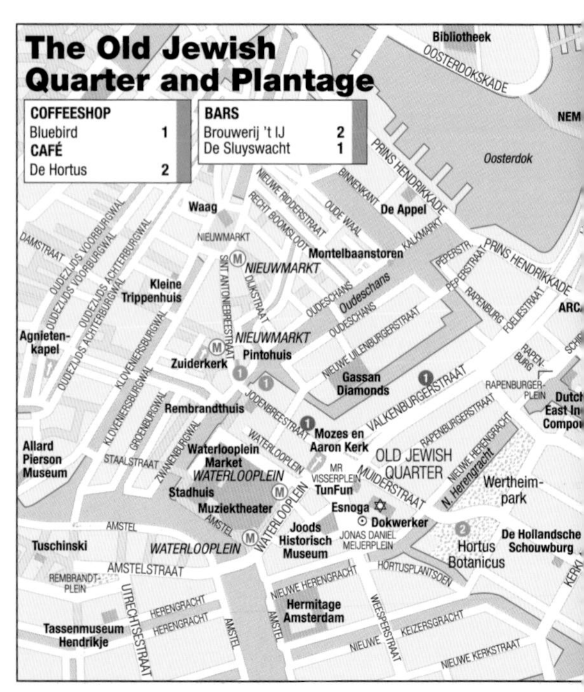

Inside, amid all the architectural mediocrity, there is one minor attraction, this being the glass columns in the public passageway towards the rear of the complex. These give a salutary lesson on the fragility of the Netherlands: two columns contain water indicating the sea levels in the Dutch towns of Vlissingen and IJmuiden (below knee height), while another records the levels experienced during the 1953 flood disaster (way above head height). At their base, a concrete pile shows what is known as "Normal Amsterdam Level" (NAP), originally calculated in 1684 as the average water level in the river IJ and still the basis for measuring altitude above sea level across Europe.

WATERLOOPLEIN

MAP PP.82–83, POCKET MAP C14–D14

The indeterminate modernity of the Stopera complex dominates **Waterlooplein**, a rectangular parcel of land that was originally swampy marsh. This was the site of the first Jewish Quarter, but by the late nineteenth century it had become an insanitary slum. The slums were cleared in the 1880s and thereafter the open spaces of the Waterlooplein hosted the largest and liveliest market in the city, the place where Jews and Gentiles met to trade. In the war, the Germans used the square to round up their victims, but despite these ugly connotations the Waterlooplein was revived in the 1950s as the site of the city's main **flea market** (Mon–Sat 9am–5pm) and remains so to this day. It's

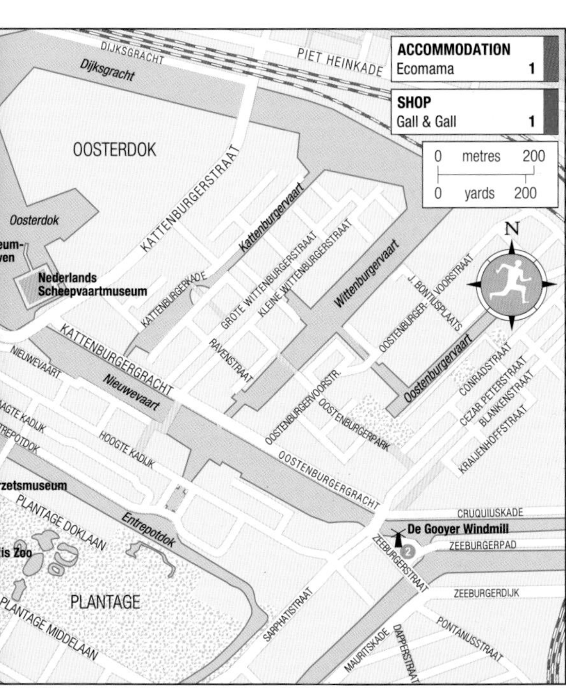

nowhere near as large as it once was, but nonetheless it's still the final resting place of many a pair of yellow corduroy flares and has some diverting antique and junk stalls to root through. If you're after a bargain, head there early, as it's very popular with tourists.

Nearby, at the very tip of Waterlooplein, where the River Amstel meets the Zwanenburgwal canal, there is a sombre **memorial** – a black stone tribute to the dead of the Jewish resistance. The inscription from Jeremiah translates, "If my eyes were a well of tears, I would cry day and night for the fallen fighters of my beloved people." Metres away, a second sculpture honours philosopher and theologian **Baruch Spinoza** who was born nearby in 1632.

MR VISSERPLEIN

MAP PP.82–83, POCKET MAP D14

Just behind the Muziektheater, on the corner of **Mr Visserplein**, is the **Mozes en Aaron Kerk**, a rather glum Neoclassical structure built on the site of a clandestine Catholic church in the 1840s. The square itself, a busy junction for traffic speeding towards the IJ tunnel, takes its name from Mr Visser, President of the Supreme Court of the Netherlands in 1939. He was dismissed the following year when the Germans occupied the country, and became an active member of the Jewish resistance, working for the illegal underground newspaper *Het Parool* ("The Password") and refusing to wear the yellow Star of David. He died in 1942, a few days after publicly – and famously – denouncing all forms of collaboration.

ESNOGA

Mr Visserplein T 020 624 5351, W esnoga.com. March–Oct Sun–Thurs 10am–5pm & Fri 10am–4pm; Nov–Feb Sun–Thurs 10am–4pm & Fri 10am–2pm; closed Yom Kippur. €15, including Joods Historich Museum (see opposite). MAP PP.82–83, POCKET MAP D14

The brown and bulky brickwork of the **Esnoga** or Portuguese synagogue was completed in 1675 for the city's Sephardic community. One of Amsterdam's most imposing buildings, it has been barely altered since its construction, its lofty interior following the Sephardic tradition in having the *Hechal* (the Ark of the Covenant) and *tebah* (from where services are led) at opposite ends. Also traditional is the seating, with two sets of wooden benches (for the men) facing each other across the central aisle – the women have separate galleries up above. A set of superb brass chandeliers holds the candles that remain the only source of artificial light. When it was completed, the synagogue was one of the largest in the world, its congregation almost certainly the richest; today, the Sephardic community has dwindled to just a few families, whose traditions are celebrated in the surrounding outhouses, from the mourning room to the rabbi's room and the intimate winter synagogue. The mystery is why the Nazis left the building alone – no one knows for sure, but it seems likely that they intended to turn it into a museum once all the Jews had been murdered.

TUNFUN

Mr Visserplein 7 ⓣ 020 689 4300, ⓦ tunfun.nl. Daily 10am–6pm. Children 1–12 €8.50, free for adults and under-1s. MAP PP.82–83, POCKET MAP D14

This large **indoor playground** near the Portuguese synagogue has lots of equipment to clamber into, under and over, and a host of kids' activities and workshops including football, gymnastics, films and trampolining. Children must be accompanied by an adult, and there's an on-site café that caters to little ones.

JONAS DANIEL MEIJERPLEIN

MAP PP.82–83, POCKET MAP F5

In the shadow of the Esnoga, **Jonas Daniel Meijerplein** is the square where, in February 1941, around four hundred Jewish men were loaded onto trucks and taken to their deaths at Mauthausen concentration camp, in reprisal for the killing of a Dutch Nazi during a street fight. The arrests sparked off the February Strike, a general strike in protest against the Germans' treatment of the Jews. It was organized by the outlawed Communist Party and spearheaded by Amsterdam's transport workers and dockers in a rare demonstration of solidarity with the Jews. The strike was quickly suppressed, but is still commemorated by an annual wreath-laying ceremony on February 25, as well as by Mari Andriessen's statue *The Dokwerker* (Dockworker) standing on the square.

JOODS HISTORISCH MUSEUM

Nieuwe Amstelstraat 1 ⓣ 020 531 0310, ⓦ jhm.nl. Daily 11am–5pm; closed Yom Kippur. €15, including Esnoga (see opposite). MAP PP.82–83, POCKET MAP D14

The **Joods Historisch Museum** (Jewish Historical Museum) is cleverly shoehorned into four adjacent Ashkenazi synagogues that date from the late seventeenth century. For years after World War II these buildings lay abandoned, but they were finally refurbished – and connected by walkways – in the 1980s, to accommodate a Jewish exhibition centre.

JOODS HISTORISCH MUSEUM

The first major display area, just beyond the reception desk on the ground floor of the Nieuwe Synagoge, features temporary exhibitions on Jewish life and culture. Upstairs is a history of Dutch Jewry from 1900 to the present. Inevitably, the emphasis is on the calamity that befell them during the German occupation of World War II, but there is also a biting display on the indifferent/hostile reaction of many Dutch men and women to liberated Jews in 1945. Moving on, the ground floor of the adjacent **Grote Synagoge** holds an engaging display on Jewish culture. There is a fine collection of religious silverware here, plus all manner of antique artefacts illustrating religious customs and practices. The gallery up above holds a finely judged social history of the country's Jewish population from 1600 to 1900.

HERMITAGE AMSTERDAM

Amstel 51 ⓣ 020 530 7488, ⓦ hermitage.nl. Daily 10am–5pm. €17.50. MAP PP.82–83, POCKET MAP F5

Backing onto the River Amstel, the stern-looking **Amstelhof** started out as a *hofje*, or almshouse for the care of elderly women, built in the 1680s on behalf of the Dutch Reformed Church. In time, it grew to fill most of the land between Nieuwe Herengracht and Nieuwe Keizersgracht, becoming a fully fledged hospital in the process, but in the 1980s it became clear that its medical facilities were out of date and it went up for sale. An ambitious scheme ensued to convert it into a museum, the **Hermitage Amsterdam**. Completed in 2009, with the historic exterior preserved and a light, modern interior, its multiple galleries now display prime pieces loaned from the Hermitage in St Petersburg. Exhibitions, which usually last about five months, have included Spanish Masters from the Hermitage and "Impressionism: Sensation & Inspiration". The museum has proved immensely popular, so much so that it has begun to diversify and in 2016 it opended a new section "Outsider Art Museum" – outsiders being untrained artists, often from psychiatric hospitals and the like.

PLANTAGE

MAP PP.82–83, POCKET MAP G5–H5

Developed in the middle of the nineteenth century, the **Plantage**, with its comfortable streets spreading to either side of the Plantage Middenlaan boulevard, was built as part of a concerted attempt to provide good-quality housing for the city's expanding middle classes. Although it was never as fashionable as the older residential parts of the Grachtengordel (see p.52), the new district did contain elegant villas and spacious terraces, making it a first suburban port of call for many aspiring Jews. Nowadays, the Plantage is still one of the more prosperous parts of the city, in a modest sort of way, and boasts two especially enjoyable attractions – the Hortus Botanicus botanical gardens and the Verzetsmuseum (Dutch Resistance Museum).

HORTUS BOTANICUS

Plantage Middenlaan 2a ⓣ 020 625 9021, ⓦ dehortus.nl. Daily 10am–5pm. €8.50. MAP PP.82–83, POCKET MAP F5–G4

Amsterdam's lush **Hortus Botanicus** was founded in 1682 as medicinal gardens for the

HORTUS BOTANICUS

use of the city's physicians and apothecaries. Thereafter, many of the city's merchants made a point of bringing back exotic species from the East, the result being the six thousand-odd plant species exhibited here today. The gardens are divided into several distinct sections, each clearly labelled and its location pinpointed by a map available at the entrance kiosk.

Most of the outdoor sections are covered by plants, trees and shrubs from the temperate and Arctic zones. There's also a three-climates glasshouse, where the plants are arranged according to their geographical origins, a capacious palm house, an orchid nursery and a butterfly house. It's all very low-key – and none the worse for that – and the gardens make a relaxing break on any tour of central Amsterdam, especially as the café, in the old orangery, serves up tasty sandwiches, coffee and cakes (see p.89).

WERTHEIMPARK

MAP PP.82–83, POCKET MAP G4

The pocket-sized **Wertheimpark**, across the road from the Hortus Botanicus, is home to the Auschwitz Monument, a simple affair with symbolically broken mirrors and an inscription that reads *Nooit meer Auschwitz* ("Auschwitz – Never Again"). It was designed by the late Dutch writer Jan Wolkers.

DE HOLLANDSCHE SCHOUWBURG

Plantage Middenlaan 24 Ⓣ 020 531 0310, Ⓦ hollandscheschouwburg.nl. Daily 11am–5pm; closed Yom Kippur. Free.
MAP PP.82–83, POCKET MAP G5

Another sad relic of the war, **De Hollandsche Schouwburg** was once a thriving Jewish theatre, but the Germans turned it into the main assembly point for Amsterdam Jews prior to their deportation. Inside, there was no daylight and families were interned in conditions that foreshadowed those of the camps they would soon be taken to. The building has been refurbished to house a small exhibition on the plight of the city's Jews, but the old auditorium out at the back has been left as an empty, roofless shell. A memorial column of basalt on a Star of David base stands where the stage once was, an intensely mournful monument to suffering of unfathomable proportions.

ARTIS ZOO

Plantage Kerklaan 38–40 ⓣ 020 523 3694, ⓦ artis.nl. Daily: March–Oct 9am–6pm; Nov–Feb 9am–5pm; June–Aug Sat until dusk. €20.50; 3- to 9-year-olds €17. MAP PP.82–83, POCKET MAP G5

Opened in 1838, **Artis Zoo** is the oldest zoo in the Netherlands and one of the city's top tourist attractions, though thankfully its layout and refreshing lack of bars and cages mean that it never feels overcrowded. Highlights include an African savanna environment, a seventy-metre-long aviary, aquaria and a South American zone with llamas and the world's largest rodent, the capybara. Feeding times – always popular – include 11am for the birds of prey; 11.30am and 3.45pm seals and sea lions; 2pm pelicans; 12.30pm crocodiles (Sun only); 3pm lions and tigers (not Thurs); and 3.30pm penguins. In addition, **Micropia** (€14, 3–9 year-olds €12) is dedicated to the secret world of micro-organisms and will appeal to any budding biologists in the family. The on-site Planetarium has five or six shows daily, all in Dutch, though you can pick up a leaflet with an English translation from the desk.

VERZETSMUSEUM

Plantage Kerklaan 61 ⓣ 020 620 2535, ⓦ verzetsmuseum.org. Mon, Sat & Sun 11am–5pm, Tues–Fri 10am–5pm, €10. MAP PP.82–83, POCKET MAP G5

The excellent **Verzetsmuseum** (Dutch Resistance Museum) outlines the development of the Dutch Resistance from the German invasion of the Netherlands in May 1940 to the country's liberation in 1945. The main themes of the occupation are dealt with honestly, noting the fine balance between cooperation and collaboration, while smaller displays focus on aspects such as the protest against the rounding-up of Amsterdam's Jews in 1941 and the so-called Milk Strike of 1943. There are fascinating old photographs and a host of original artefacts including examples of illegal newsletters and, chillingly, signed German death warrants. The museum also has dozens of little metal sheets providing biographical sketches of the members of the Resistance.

THE VERZETSMUSEUM

Shop

GALL & GALL

Jodenbreestraat 23 ⓣ 020 428 7060, ⓦ gall.nl. Mon–Fri 10am–10pm.
MAP PP.82–83, POCKET MAP D13

Has an outstanding range of Dutch *jenevers* (gins) and flavoured spirits as well as a good selection of imported wine, champagne and prosecco. Part of the largest chain of wine merchants in Amsterdam.

Coffeshop

BLUEBIRD

Sint Antoniesbreestraat 71 ⓣ 020 622 5232. Daily 9.30am–1am. MAP PP.82–83, POCKET MAP D13

Popular coffeeshop with sink-in sofas and tall stools. The *Bluebird* also serves food, coffees and other non-alcoholic drinks, and you can get your smoking fix here too.

Café

DE HORTUS

Plantage Middenlaan 2a ⓣ 020 625 9021, ⓦ dehostus.nl. Daily 10am–4.30pm.
MAP PP.82–83, POCKET MAP F5

Tucked away amid the luxuriant greenery of the Hortus Botanicus (see p.86), this family-orientated café (mind the buggies) occupies a spacious former orangery. They serve up good, tangy coffee, filling sandwiches and freshly made rolls. But, whatever you do, save space for the desserts in general and the cheesecake in particular: the raspberry cheesecake may well be the best north of the Alps.

DE HORTUS

Bars

BROUWERIJ 'T IJ

De Gooyer windmill, Funenkade 7 ⓣ 020 622 8325, ⓦ brouwerijhetij.nl. Daily 2–8pm.
MAP PP.82–83, POCKET MAP H5

Well-established if somewhat frugal bar and mini-brewery in the old public baths adjoining the De Gooyer windmill. Serves up an excellent range of beers and ales, from the thunderously strong Columbus amber ale (9%) to the creamier, more soothing Natte (6.5%).

DE SLUYSWACHT

Jodenbreestraat 1 ⓣ 020 625 7611, ⓦ sluyswacht.nl. Mon–Thurs 12.30pm–1am, Fri & Sat 12.30pm–3am, Sun 12.30–7pm.
MAP PP.82–83, POCKET MAP D13

This pleasant little bar occupies an old and now solitary gabled house by the lock gates opposite the Rembrandthuis. A smashing spot to nurse a beer on a warm summer's night, gazing down the canal towards the Montelbaanstoren.

The eastern docklands and Amsterdam Noord

Amsterdam's docklands once extended right along the south side of the River IJ, comprising a vast maritime complex incorporating both the Westerdok (western docklands, see p.75) and the Oosterdok (eastern docklands). Industrial decline began during the 1880s, but the docklands' assorted artificial islands are now being redefined as residential and leisure districts with some startling modern architecture – balanced by two reminders of the Oosterdok's nautical heyday, the warehouses of Entrepotdok and the engaging Scheepvaartmuseum (Maritime Museum). Reached by ferry, the former shipyards and commercial buildings of Amsterdam Noord, on the north side of the IJ, are in an earlier phase of redevelopment, but the slab of land opposite Centraal Station has been transformed by the construction of the EYE Film Institute, Amsterdam's best cinema in the city's proudest new building. Further out along the north side of the river, there's a second patch of cutting-edge regeneration in the former NDSM Shipyard, now a creative arts and events hub.

OOSTERDOK

MAP PP.92–93, POCKET MAP H3–H4

Stretching east from Centraal Station lies the **Oosterdok**, or **eastern docklands**, whose network of artificial islands was dredged out of the River IJ to increase Amsterdam's shipping facilities in the seventeenth and eighteenth centuries. By the 1980s, this mosaic of docks, jetties and islands had become something of a post-industrial eyesore, but since then an ambitious redevelopment programme has turned things around. Easily the most agreeable way of reaching the Oosterdok is via the footbridge at the north end of Plantage Kerklaan – and metres from the Verzetsmuseum (see p.88) – which leads onto Entrepotdok.

ENTREPOTDOK

MAP PP.92–93, POCKET MAP G4–G5

Over the footbridge at the end of Plantage Kerklaan lies one of the more interesting of the Oosterdok islands, a slender rectangle whose southern quayside, **Entrepotdok**, is lined by a long series of nineteenth-century gabled warehouses that were once part of the largest warehouse complex in continental Europe. Each warehouse sports the name of a town or island; goods for onward transportation were stored in the appropriate warehouse until there were enough to fill a boat or barge. The warehouses have been converted into offices and apartments, a fate that must surely befall the buildings of the central East India Company compound, at the west end of Entrepotdok on Kadijksplein.

SCHEEPVAARTMUSEUM

Kattenburgerplein ⓣ 020 523 2222, ⓦ hetscheepvaartmuseum.nl. Daily 9am–5pm. €15. MAP PP.92–93, POCKET MAP G4

One of the city's most popular attractions, the **Scheepvaartmuseum** (Maritime Museum) occupies the old arsenal of the Dutch navy, a vast sandstone structure built on the Oosterdok in the seventeenth century. Visitors get their bearings in the central **courtyard** from where you can enter any one of three display areas – labelled "West", "Noord" and "Oost". Of the three, the **West** displays are the most child-orientated, the **Oost** the most substantial, including garish ships' figureheads, examples of early atlases and navigational equipment. There are many nautical paintings in this section too, some devoted to the achievements of Dutch trading ships, others showing heavy seas and shipwrecks and yet more celebrating the successes of the Dutch navy, the most powerful fleet in the world from the 1650s to the 1680s. Willem van de Velde II (1633–1707) was the most successful of the Dutch marine painters of the period and there's a small sample of his work here.

The "**Noord**" section features a couple of short nautical films and also gives access to the 78-metre De Amsterdam, a full-scale replica of an East Indiaman merchant ship. The original vessel first set sail in 1748, but came to an ignominious end, getting stuck on the English coast near Hastings. Visitors can wander the ship's decks, galleys, storerooms and gun bays at their leisure.

OOSTERDOK

MUSEUMHAVEN

Oosterdok. Open access. Free. MAP P.92–93, POCKET MAP G3

Moored on the long jetty leading up to the giant green hood above the IJ tunnel are the antique boats and barges of the **Museumhaven**, which together make an informal record of the development of local shipping; the earliest boats date from the middle of the nineteenth century, and plaques, in English and Dutch, give the historical lowdown on the more important vessels.

NEMO

Oosterdok ☎ 020 531 3233, Ⓦ nemosciencemuseum.nl. Tues–Sun 10am–5.30pm, plus Mon 10am–5.30pm during school hols incl. July–Aug. €15. MAP PP.92–93, POCKET MAP G3

Much of the distinctive elevated hood above the IJ tunnel is occupied by the **NEMO** centre, a (pre-teenage) kids' attraction par excellence, with all sorts of interactive science and technological exhibits spread over six floors and set out under several broad themes.

DE APPEL

Prins Hendrikkade 142 ☎ 020 625 5651, Ⓦ deappel.nl. Tues–Sun 11am–6pm. €7. MAP PP.92–93, POCKET MAP F3

A self-styled international institution for contemporary art, the **De Appel** arts centre offers a flamboyant programme of temporary exhibitions in a variety of media, from film through to sculpture, installations and paintings. The nineteenth-century premises have had a patchy history – they have previously served as both a spiritual and a meditation centre – but they

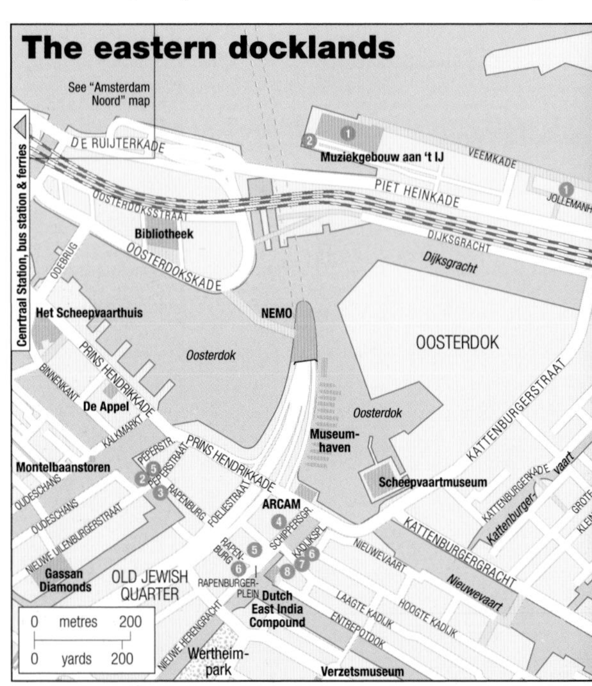

NEMO

are large enough to showcase several exhibitions at any one time and there are also performances, lectures and debates.

BIBLIOTHEEK

Oosterdokskade 143 ⓣ 020 523 0900, ⓦ oba.nl. Daily 10am–10pm. MAP PP.92–93, POCKET MAP F2

Across the harbour-spanning footbridge from **NEMO**, Amsterdam's principal Bibliotheek (Library) occupies a cleverly designed modern block that was opened in 2007. The building was designed by Jo Coenon, a Dutch architect and urban planner of repute, and the spacious, subtly lit interior spreads over ten floors; among much else, it includes an auditorium, an exhibition room and a terrace café, which is a popular spot for students to chew the academic cud.

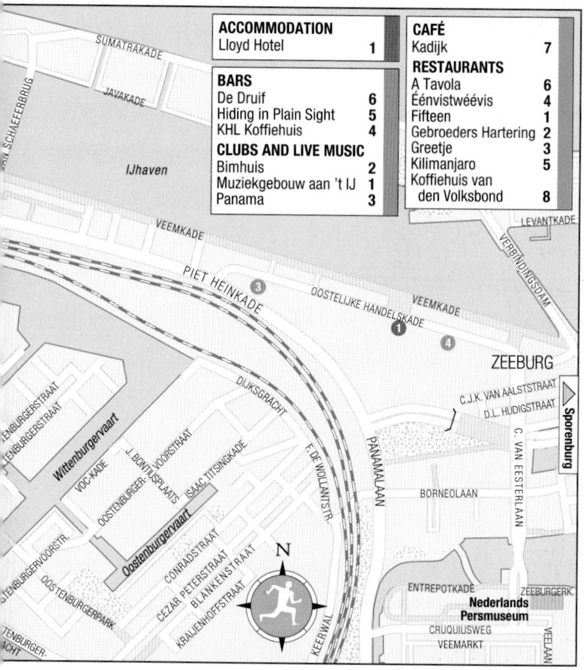

ACCOMMODATION
Lloyd Hotel 1

BARS
De Druif 6
Hiding in Plain Sight 5
KHL Koffiehuis 4

CLUBS AND LIVE MUSIC
Bimhuis 2
Muziekgebouw aan 't IJ 1
Panama 3

CAFÉ
Kadijk 7

RESTAURANTS
A Tavola 6
Éénvistwéévis 4
Fifteen 1
Gebroeders Hartering 2
Greetje 3
Kilimanjaro 5
Koffiehuis van den Volksbond 8

ZEEBURG

MUZIEKGEBOUW AAN 'T IJ

Piet Heinkade 1 020 788 2000, muziekgebouw.nl. No fixed opening times – open for performances. MAP PP.92–93, POCKET MAP G2

One of the Oosterdok's prime buildings, the **Muziekgebouw** is a high-spec, multipurpose music auditorium overlooking the River IJ. It encompasses two medium-sized concert halls, a café and a bar. It also has state-of-the-art acoustics, and has given real impetus to the redevelopment going on along the IJ. As well as some contemporary music, it has a good programme of opera and orchestral music which brings a rather highbrow crowd to this part of town. It's worth a visit for the building alone.

ZEEBURG

MAP PP.92–93, POCKET MAP H5

To the north and east of the Oosterdok, **Zeeburg** – basically the old docklands between the Muziekgebouw and **Java** and **KNSM** islands – is one of the city's most up-and-coming districts. Actually a series of artificial islands and peninsulas connected by bridges, the docks here date to the end of the nineteenth century. By the early 1990s, the area was virtually derelict, so the council began a massive renovation, which has been going on for nearly two decades. This is now the fastest-developing part of Amsterdam, with a mixture of renovated dockside structures and new landmark buildings that give it a modern (and very watery) feel that's markedly different from the city centre – despite being just a ten-minute walk from Centraal Station. Explore the area by **bike**, especially as distances are, at least in Amsterdam terms, comparatively large – from the Muziekgebouw to the east end of KNSM Island is about 4km.

Alternatively, there are two useful transport connections from Centraal Station: tram #26 to Sporenburg island via Piet Heinkade and bus #48 to Java Island and KNSM Island.

NEDERLANDS PERSMUSEUM

Zeeburgerkade 10 020 692 8810, persmuseum.nl. Tues–Fri 10am–5pm & Sun noon–5pm. €7. MAP PP.92–93, POCKET MAP H4

From Centraal Station, take tram #26 to the Rietlandpark stop near the west end of Sporenburg island, from near where C van Eesterenlaan slices south, cutting along the edge of two old harbours to Zeeburgerkade, which is home to the **Nederlands Persmuseum**. The museum has a mildly interesting series of displays on the leading Dutch newspapermen of yesteryear, beginning with Abraham Casteleyn, who first published a combined business and political newssheet in the 1650s. Of more immediate interest are the cartoons, often vitriolic attacks on those in power both here and elsewhere; for instance, one recent premier – Jan Peter Balkenende – is often mockingly portrayed as Harry Potter (he looks like him).

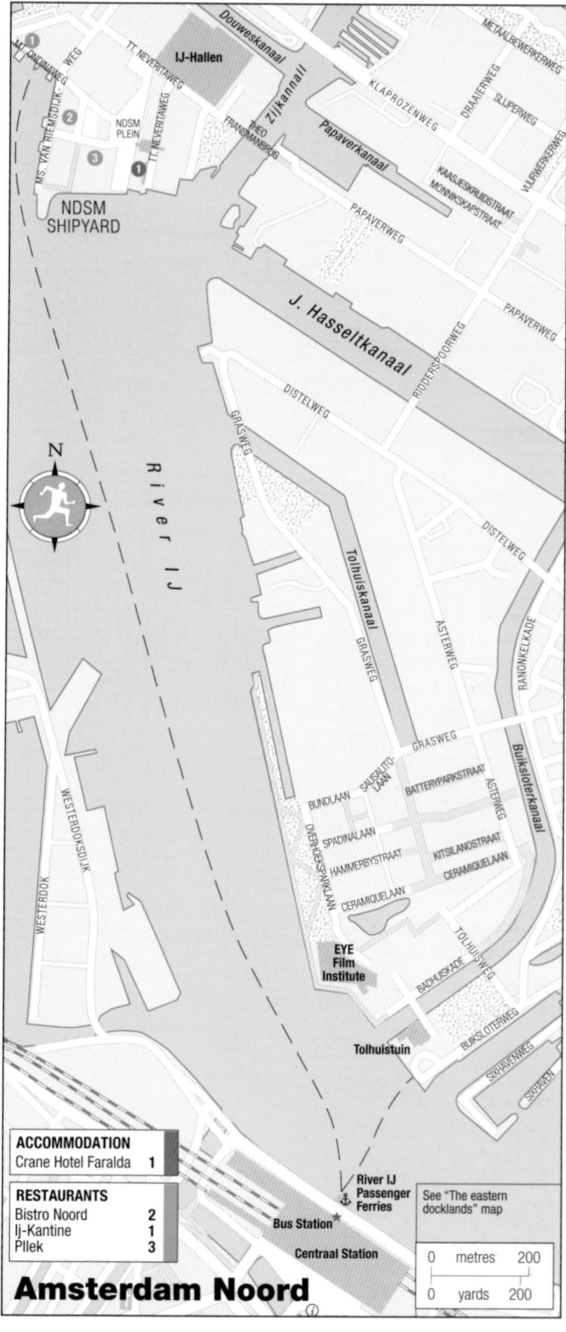
Amsterdam Noord
ACCOMMODATION
Crane Hotel Faralda 1
RESTAURANTS
Bistro Noord 2
Ij-Kantine 1
Pllek 3
IJ-Hallen
NDSM PLEIN
NDSM SHIPYARD
Douweskanaal
Zijkanaal I
Papaverkanaal
J. Hasseltkanaal
Tolhuiskanaal
Buiksloterkanaal
River IJ
EYE Film Institute
Tolhuistuin
River IJ Passenger Ferries
Bus Station
Centraal Station
See "The eastern docklands" map
0 metres 200
0 yards 200

PUBLIC ART AT NDSM SHIPYARD

EYE FILM INSTITUTE

IJpromenade 1 ⓣ 020 589 1400, ⓦ eyefilm.nl. Exhibition space daily 10am–7pm. €11. Take the GVB Buiksloterwegveer passenger ferry across the River IJ from the back of Centraal Station (every 10–15min; 5min; free); it's a 5min walk from the ferry dock. MAP P.95, POCKET MAP E1

Clearly visible from the south side of the River IJ, the **EYE Film Institute** occupies a superb new building, a graceful shimmering structure whose sleek, angular lines were designed by a Viennese architecture firm, Delugan Meissl. The EYE offers engaging views back over both the river and the city centre from all its three floors, which hold a bar-restaurant, a shop, a film-focused library and four cinema screens showing an enterprising programme of classic and cult films. There is also an exhibition area offering four major displays each year.

NDSM SHIPYARD

Take the GVB passenger ferry service across the River IJ from the back of Centraal Station (every 30–40min; 15min; free). MAP P.95, POCKET MAP E1

Until it closed in 1979, the **NDSM Shipyard** was a key part of Amsterdam's industrial economy, its workshops, wharves and engineering plant spreading over a large chunk of land on the north side of the River IJ. After NDSM's demise, no one was quite sure what to do with the site, but very little was demolished and in the last few years the old shipyard – and its distressed industrial buildings – has been revived as an arts and events hub, with a platoon of new or recycled buildings, plus hotels and restaurants.

The Dutch East India Company

Founded in 1602, the Dutch East India Company (the VOC – Verenigde Oostindische Compagnie) imported spices to Europe from India, Sri Lanka, Indochina, Malaya, China, Japan and modern-day Indonesia. For nearly two hundred years the VOC was the chief pillar of Amsterdam's wealth, but, expelled from most of the best trading stations by the British and in heavy debt, Napoleon had little time for its privileges and pretensions – he abolished its ruling council and ultimately dissolved the company in 1799.

Café

KADIJK

Kadijksplein 5 ⓣ 0617 744 411. Mon–Thurs & Sun 4pm–1am, Fri & Sat 4pm–3am; kitchen till 10pm. MAP PP.92–93, POCKET MAP G4

Tiny place which – contrary to what the homely interior with Delft blue crockery might suggest – has an excellent Indonesian inspired menu. Tasty chicken or beef *saté* goes for €15. For dessert try the traditional Indonesian *spekkoek* (spiced cake) served with coffee.

Restaurants

A TAVOLA

Kadijksplein 9 ⓣ 020 625 4994, ⓦ atavolarestaurant.nl. Daily noon–3pm & 5.30–10.30pm. MAP PP.92–93, POCKET MAP G4

On a pleasant canalside square, this attractive restaurant serves up simple but delicious Italian food, including a first-rate selection of antipasti, pasta, meat and fish. Mains average around €25.

BISTRO NOORD

Ondinaweg 32 ⓣ 020 705 9906, ⓦ bistronoord.nl. Daily noon–4pm & 6–10pm. MAP P.95, POCKET MAP E1

Amsterdam Noord hotspot featuring French cooking with an emphasis on seafood – particularly oysters – and a Texas smoker for meat (two-course lunch €27.50). The interior is airy and industrial, with crate-wood floors and high ceilings.

ÉÉNVISTWÉÉVIS

Schippersgracht 6. ⓣ 020 623 2894, ⓦ eenvistweevis.nl. Tues–Sat 6–10pm. MAP PP.92–93, POCKET MAP G4

A great fish restaurant serving an interesting selection of seafood, such as seabass with rosemary and thyme complemented by well-chosen wines. Mains around €25.

FIFTEEN

Jollemanshof 9 ⓣ 020 509 5015, ⓦ fifteen.nl. Daily 5.30–11pm. MAP PP.92–93, POCKET MAP H2

The Amsterdam branch of Jamie Oliver's successful restaurant formula, which annually gives a bunch of youngsters the chance to work in a top-notch kitchen. The food sticks to the Oliver template with a menu described as "modern Mediterranean with Italian influences" – expect lots of fresh olives and buffalo

JAMIE OLIVER'S FIFTEEN

mozzarella to start followed by imaginative pasta (truffle and egg yolk ravioli) and risotto dishes, plus daily changing meat and fish mains (from €24).

GEBROEDERS HARTERING

Peperstraat 10 ⓣ 020 421 0699, ⓦ gebr-hartering.nl. Tues & Wed 6–10.30pm, Thurs–Sat 6–11pm, Sun 6–10pm. MAP PP.92–93, POCKET MAP F4

Run by two brothers, *Gebroeders Hartering* is a special occasion sort of place. Choose from four courses for €40 up to nine courses for €75. Menus are always seasonal and often adventurous, with offal and unpasteurized cheeses frequently appearing.

GREETJE

Peperstraat 23 ⓣ 020 779 7450, ⓦ restaurantgreetje.nl. Daily 6–10pm. MAP PP.92–93, POCKET MAP F4

A cosy, busy restaurant that serves up Dutch staples with a modern twist. A changing menu (mains around €25) reflects the seasons and the favourite dishes of the owner's mother – a native of the southern Netherlands. Superb home-cooking in a great atmosphere.

GREETJE

IJ-KANTINE

Ondinaweg 15–17 ⓣ 020 633 7162, ⓦ ijkantine.nl. Daily 9am–10pm; bar till midnight. MAP P.95, POCKET MAP E1

Large, canteen-like restaurant and bar in a one-time industrial building a few paces from the ferry dock. Serves up a please-all menu of burgers (€14.50), pasta and the like to a mainly local crew.

KILIMANJARO

Rapenburgerplein 6 ⓣ 020 622 3485, ⓦ kilimanjarorestaurant.nl. Tues–Sun 5–10pm. MAP PP.92–93, POCKET MAP G4

African restaurant in a largely forgotten part of town, serving the likes of West African antelope goulash, Moroccan *tajine* and crocodile steak. Vegetarian options available. Moderately priced and super-friendly.

KOFFIEHUIS VAN DEN VOLKSBOND

Kadijksplein 4 ⓣ 020 622 1209, ⓦ koffiehuisvandenvolksbond.nl. Daily 6–10pm. MAP PP.92–93, POCKET MAP G4

Once a dockworkers' café, this is now a popular Oosterdok café-restaurant. The eclectic menu manages to pack in everything from fresh artichoke with mustard as a starter (€7.50) to Moroccan-style lamb and Cajun gumbo mains (€16.50).

PLLEK

Tt. Neveritaweg 59 ⓣ 020 290 0020, ⓦ pllek.nl. Mon–Thurs & Sun 9.30am–1am, Fri & Sat 9.30am–3am. MAP P.95, POCKET MAP E1

One of several hipster places to have sprung up at the NDSM wharf, *Pllek* is arguably the best. Dishes are inventive, international and affordable: mains like wild boar stew will set you back around €19.

Bars

DE DRUIF

Rapenburgerplein 83 ⓣ 020 624 4530. Daily 3pm–1am, Fri & Sat until 2am. MAP PP.92–93, POCKET MAP G4

"The Grape" is one of the city's oldest bars (dating from 1631), and certainly one of its more beguiling. A popular neighbourhood joint, it pulls in an easy-going crowd.

HIDING IN PLAIN SIGHT

Rapenburg 18 ⓣ 062 529 3620, ⓦ hpsamsterdam.com. Mon–Thurs 6pm–1am, Fri & Sat 6pm–3am. MAP PP.92–93, POCKET MAP F4

Perhaps the best cocktail bar in Amsterdam, *Hiding in Plain Sight* is decorated in the style of an American speakeasy. The drinks menu is ever-changing, but always includes a large selection of Mezcal.

KHL KOFFIEHUIS

Oostelijke Handelskade 44 ⓣ 020 779 1575, ⓦ denieuwekhl.nl. Tues–Sun noon–1am. MAP PP.92–93, POCKET MAP H3

Old-fashioned coffeehouse (not to be confused with coffeeshop) with wooden panelling and heavy red curtains, located in a 1917 historic building. Small and modest menu and regular live music.

Clubs and live music

BIMHUIS

Piet Heinkade 3 ⓣ 020 788 2150, ⓦ bimhuis.nl. Daily 6.30pm–1am. MAP PP.92–93, POCKET MAP G2

The city's premier jazz and improvised music venue is located right next to the Muziekgebouw, beside the River IJ. The *Bimhuis* showcases gigs from Dutch and international artists throughout the week, as well as jam sessions and workshops. There's also a bar and restaurant with pleasant views over the river.

PANAMA

MUZIEKGEBOUW AAN 'T IJ

Piet Heinkade 1 ⓣ 020 788 2000, ⓦ muziekgebouw.nl. MAP PP.92–93, POCKET MAP G2

Located in a modern glass building overlooking the river, the *Muziekgebouw* showcases everything from classical through to jazz and rock, and has studios, rehearsal space and convention facilities.

PANAMA

Oostelijke Handelskade 4 ⓣ 020 311 8686, ⓦ panama.nl. Daily noon–1am, 3am at weekends. MAP PP.92–93, POCKET MAP H2

All-in-one restaurant, bar and nightclub located in the former power plant perched right on the river IJ. Many live performances as well as internationally renowned DJs on weekends. One of the coolest spots in the city, *Panama* has played a leading role in spicing up the Eastern docklands.

The Museum Quarter and around

During the nineteenth century, Amsterdam grew beyond its restraining canals, gobbling up the surrounding countryside with a slew of new, mostly residential suburbs. One result was the creation of Museumplein, a large triangular open space surrounded by the cream of the city's museums. The largest is the Rijksmuseum, which occupies a huge late nineteenth-century edifice overlooking the Singelgracht and possesses an exceptional collection of art and applied art. Close by, the more modern Van Gogh Museum boasts the finest assortment of Van Gogh paintings in the world, while the adjacent Stedelijk Museum has an outstanding collection of modern art. Out on this side of the city also is the Vondelpark, Amsterdam's largest and most attractive green space, whose gently landscaped rectangle of lawns and paths, lakes and streams provides the perfect place for a lazy picnic between museums. The leafy streets around the park, such as PC Hooftstraat, also provide some of the most upmarket shopping in Amsterdam.

MUSEUMPLEIN

MAP P.102, POCKET MAP C7

Extending south from Stadhouderskade to Van Baerlestraat, **Museumplein**'s wide lawns and gravelled spaces are used for a variety of outdoor activities, from visiting circuses to political demonstrations. There's a **war memorial** here too – it's the group of slim steel blocks about three-quarters of the way down the Museumplein on the left-hand side. It commemorates the women and children of the wartime concentration camps, particularly those who died at Ravensbruck.

WAR MEMORIAL, MUSEUMPLEIN

THE RIJKSMUSEUM ATRIUM

RIJKSMUSEUM

Museumstraat 1 ⓣ 020 674 7000, ⓦ rijksmuseum.nl. Daily 9am–5pm. €17.50. MAP P.102, POCKET MAP C6

The **Rijksmuseum** is without question the country's foremost museum, with one of the world's most comprehensive collections of seventeenth-century Dutch paintings, including twenty or so of **Rembrandt**'s works, plus a healthy sample of canvases by his contemporaries. These paintings from Amsterdam's Golden Age are the museum's main pull, but the Rijksmuseum also also owns an extravagant collection of paintings from every other pre-twentieth-century period of Dutch art – and has a vast hoard of applied art and sculpture. All are now shown to best advantage, following the 2013 completion of a thoroughgoing **refurbishment** that cost millions of euros. Bear in mind, though, that queues can be long, especially in summer and at weekends, so try to book online ahead of time, or come early in the morning.

Above all, it's the seventeenth-century paintings that catch the eye. There are paintings by Rembrandt's pupils – Ferdinand Bol, Gerard Dou and Gabriel Metsu; several wonderful canvases by Frans Hals, such as his scatological *Merry Drinker*; the cool interiors of Gerard ter Borch and Pieter de Hooch; soft, tonal river scenes by the Haarlem artist Salomon van Ruysdael and by Albert Cuyp; the urbane church interiors of Pieter Saenredam; the popular carousing peasants of Jan Steen; and the dreamy realism of Vermeer, as exemplified by the exquisite, lost-in-thought *Milkmaid* of 1660. However, it's the Rembrandts that steal the show, especially *The Night Watch* of 1642 – perhaps the most famous and probably the most valuable of all the artist's pictures – plus other key works, such as a late *Self-Portrait*, a touching depiction of his cowled son, *Titus*, the arresting *Staalmeesters* and *The Jewish Bride*, one of his very last pictures, finished in 1667.

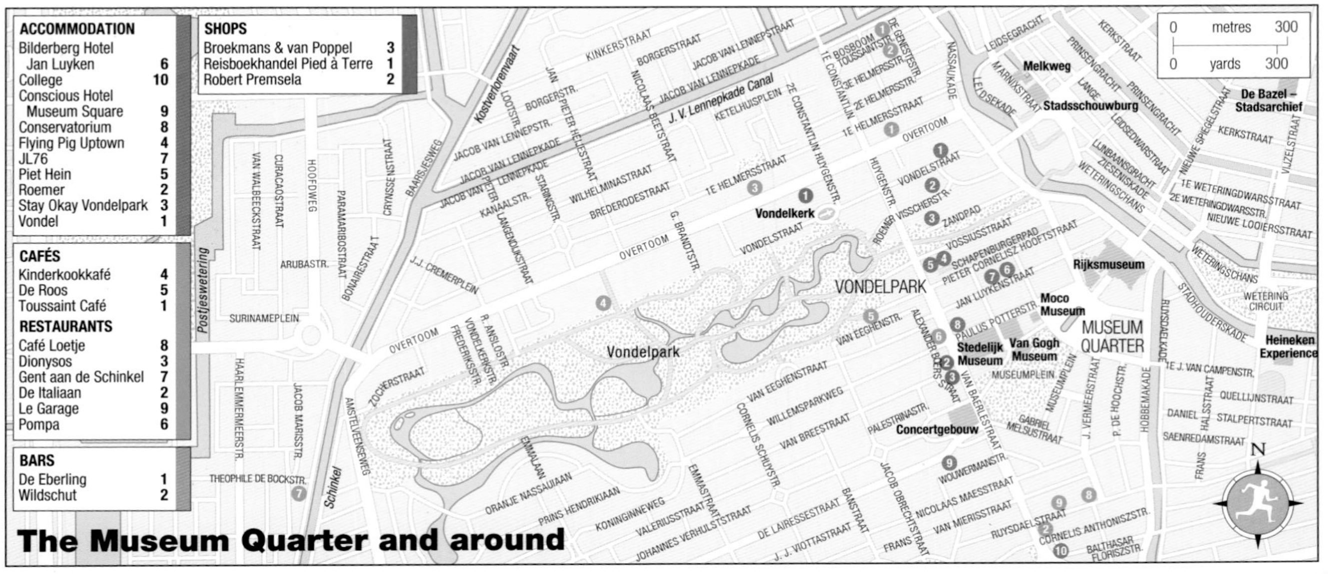
The Museum Quarter and around
ACCOMMODATION
Bilderberg Hotel Jan Luyken 6
College 10
Conscious Hotel Museum Square 9
Conservatorium 8
Flying Pig Uptown 4
JL76 7
Piet Hein 5
Roemer 2
Stay Okay Vondelpark 3
Vondel 1
SHOPS
Broekmans & van Poppel 3
Reisboekhandel Pied à Terre 1
Robert Premsela 2
CAFÉS
Kinderkookkafé 4
De Roos 5
Toussaint Café 1
RESTAURANTS
Café Loetje 8
Dionysos 3
Gent aan de Schinkel 7
De Italiaan 2
Le Garage 9
Pompa 6
BARS
De Eberling 1
Wildschut 2
0 metres 300
0 yards 300
N
Melkweg
Stadsschouwburg
De Bazel – Stadsarchief
Rijksmuseum
Moco Museum
Van Gogh Museum
Stedelijk Museum
MUSEUM QUARTER
Heineken Experience
Concertgebouw
Vondelkerk
VONDELPARK
Vondelpark
J. V. Lennepkade Canal
Kostverlorenvaart
Postjeswetering
Schinkel
OVERTOOM
NASSAUKADE
LEIDSEGRACHT
PRINSENGRACHT
KERKSTRAAT
STADHOUDERSKADE
WETERINGSCHANS
WETERING CIRCUIT
HOBBEMAKADE
RUYSDAELKADE
VAN BAERLESTRAAT
MUSEUMPLEIN
PIETER CORNELISZ HOOFTSTRAAT
JAN LUYKENSTRAAT
PAULUS POTTERSTR.
AMSTELVEENSEWEG
HOOFDWEG
SURINAMEPLEIN
HAARLEMMERMEERSTR.
EMMALAAN
KONINGINNEWEG
DE LAIRESSESTRAAT
CORNELIS SCHUYTSTR.
VAN EEGHENSTRAAT
WILLEMSPARKWEG
VAN BREESTRAAT
JACOB OBRECHTSTRAAT
VOSSIUSSTRAAT
VONDELSTRAAT
KINKERSTRAAT

MOCO MUSEUM

Honthorststraat 20 ⓣ 020 370 1997, ⓦ mocomuseum.com. Daily 10–6pm. $12.50. MAP P.102, POCKET MAP B7

The Museum Quarter has burnished its artistic credentials with the newly-opened **Moco Museum**, which is devoted to contemporary art. In a substantial, early twentieth-century brick building close to the Van Gogh Museum, its opening exhibition featured Banksy and Warhol.

VAN GOGH MUSEUM

Museumplein 6 ⓣ 020 570 5200, ⓦ vangoghmuseum.nl. Core hours: daily 9am–5pm, Fri till 10pm. €17, under 18 free. MAP P.102, POCKET MAP B7

The **Van Gogh Museum**, comprising a fabulous collection of the artist's (1853–90) work, is one of Amsterdam's top attractions. The museum occupies two buildings, with the museum entrance to the rear via the ultra-modern curved annexe, which was financed by a Japanese insurance company – the same conglomerate that paid $35 million for one of van Gogh's *Sunflowers* canvases in 1987 – and provides temporary exhibition space. A ground-floor escalator connects the annexe with the main museum building, an angular structure designed by a leading light of the De Stijl movement, Gerrit Rietveld, and opened to the public in 1973. Beautifully presented and recently renovated, this part of the museum provides an introduction to the man and his art based on paintings that were mostly inherited from Vincent's art-dealer brother Theo. There are usually small supporting displays here too, mostly putting van Gogh into artistic context with the work of his friends and contemporaries: the museum owns paintings by the likes of Toulouse-Lautrec, Cézanne, Bernard, Seurat, Gauguin, Anton Mauve, Charles Daubigny, Pissarro and Monet.

All of van Gogh's key paintings are featured in the Rietveld building, displayed chronologically, starting with the dark, sombre works of the early years such as *The Potato Eaters* and finishing up with the asylum years at St Rémy and the final, tortured paintings done at Auvers, where van Gogh lodged for the last three months of his life, before his suicide. It was at Auvers that van Gogh painted the frantic *Wheatfield with Crows* and the disturbing *Tree Roots*.

THE VAN GOGH MUSEUM

THE STEDELIJK MUSEUM

Museumplein 10 020 573 2911, stedelijk.nl. Daily 10am–6pm, Fri until 10pm. €15. MAP P.102, POCKET MAP B7

The **Stedelijk Museum** has long been Amsterdam's number one venue for modern and contemporary art and design, and finally, after moving hither and thither, it returned to its original home on Museumplein in 2012 – but its original home with a difference: the nineteenth-century building has been entirely refurbished and attached to it now is a cumbersome new extension, derisively nicknamed "the bath tub". Inside, the museum focuses on cutting-edge, **temporary exhibitions** of modern art, from photography and video through to sculpture and collage, and these are supplemented by a regularly rotated selection from the museum's large and wide-ranging **permanent collection**. Among many highlights is a particularly large sample of the work of **Piet Mondriaan** (1872–1944), from his early, muddy abstracts to the boldly coloured rectangular blocks for which he's most famous. The Stedelijk is also strong on **Kasimir Malevich** (1878–1935), whose dense attempts at Cubism lead to the dynamism and bold, primary tones of his "Suprematist" paintings – slices, blocks and bolts of colour that shift around as if about to resolve themselves into some complex computer graphic. Other high spots include several **Marc Chagall** paintings and a number of works by American Abstract Expressionists Mark Rothko, Ellsworth Kelly and Barnett Newman, plus the odd piece by Lichtenstein, Warhol, Robert Ryman, Kooning and Jean Dubuffet.

CONCERTGEBOUW

Concertgebouwplein 10 020 573 0573; box office 020 671 8345, concertgebouw.nl. English-language guided tours: Sun 12.30–1.45pm, Mon 5–6.15pm & Wed 1.30–2.45pm. €10. MAP P.102, POCKET MAP B7

The **Concertgebouw** (Concert Hall) is the home of the famed – and much recorded – Koninklijk (Royal) Concertgebouw Orchestra. When the German composer Brahms visited Amsterdam in the 1870s he was scathing about the locals' lack of culture and in particular their lack of

THE STEDELIJK MUSEUM

an even halfway suitable venue for his music. In the face of such ridicule, a consortium of Amsterdam businessmen got together to fund the construction of a brand-new concert hall and the result was the Concertgebouw, completed in 1888. Since then it has become renowned among musicians and concertgoers for its marvellous acoustics, and after a facelift and the replacement of its crumbling foundations in the early 1990s it is looking and sounding better than ever. The acoustics of the Grote Zaal (Large Hall) are unparalleled, and the smaller Kleine Zaal regularly hosts chamber concerts. Prices vary enormously depending on who is appearing as well as the type of seat; tickets start at around €25.

Tours last a little over an hour and take in the Grote Zaal, the Kleine Zaal, and the various backroom activities behind all this – control rooms, piano stores, dressing rooms and the like.

VONDELPARK

Several entrances off Van Baerlestraat hetvondelpark.net. Daily dawn to dusk. Free. MAP P.102, POCKET MAP A7

Amsterdam is short of green spaces, which makes the leafy expanses of the **Vondelpark**, a short stretch from Museumplein and the Concertgebouw, doubly welcome. This is easily the largest and most popular of the city's parks, its network of footpaths used by a healthy slice of the city's population. The park dates back to 1864, when a group of leading Amsterdammers clubbed together to transform the soggy marshland that lay beyond the Leidsepoort into a landscaped park. The park possesses over

THE VONDELPARK

one hundred species of tree, a wide variety of local and imported plants, and – among many incidental features – a bandstand, an excellent rose garden and a network of ponds and narrow waterways that are home to many sorts of wildfowl. There are other animals too: cows, sheep, hundreds of squirrels, plus a large colony of bright-green (and very noisy) parakeets. During the summer the park regularly hosts free concerts and theatrical performances, mostly in its own specially designed open-air theatre.

The park is named after Amsterdam's foremost poet, **Joost van den Vondel** (1587–1679), who ran a hosiery business here in the city, in between writing and hobnobbing with the local elite. Vondel was a kind of Dutch Shakespeare and his *Gijsbrecht van Amstel*, in which he celebrates Dutch life during the Golden Age, is one of the classics of Dutch literature. There's a large and somewhat grandiose statue of the man on a plinth near the main entrance to the park.

Shops

BROEKMANS & VAN POPPEL

Van Baerlestraat 92–94 ⓣ 020 679 6576, ⓦ broekmans.com. Mon–Fri 9am–6pm, Sat 9am–5pm. MAP P.102, POCKET MAP B7

With a name like that you'd expect something highbrow, and so it proves: these experts in classical music and opera have perhaps the best selection in the city of CDs and DVDs, though their real speciality is sheet music, both new and secondhand.

REISBOEKHANDEL PIED À TERRE

Overtoom 135 ⓣ 020 627 4455, ⓦ jvw.nl. Mon 1–6pm, Tues–Fri 10am–6pm, Thurs until 9pm, Sat 10am–5pm. MAP P.102, POCKET MAP A6

The city's best travel bookshop has knowledgeable staff and a huge selection of books, road maps and various globes. Their wide range of international hiking maps is worth seeking out too.

ROBERT PREMSELA

Van Baerlestraat 78 ⓣ 020 662 4266, ⓦ premsela.nl. Mon noon–6pm, Tues–Fri 10am–6pm, Sat 10am–5.30pm, Sun 11am–5pm. MAP P.102, POCKET MAP B7

This long-established bookshop has a number of specialisms, including architecture and photography, though art in general – and Dutch art in particular – comes top of the bibliographic pile. As you might expect, most books are in Dutch, but there is a good range of English titles as well.

Cafés

KINDERKOOKKAFÉ

Vondelpark 6b (Overtoom 325) ⓣ 020 625 3257, ⓦ kinderkookkafe.nl. Daily 10am–5pm. MAP P.102, POCKET MAP A6

REISBOEKHANDEL PIED À TERRE

A café run by children aged 5–12, who cook, wait and wash dishes. Though this may sound like a recipe for disaster, the food – pizzas, sandwiches, cakes – is simple and (usually) tasty, and it's all good fun. Booking essential at the weekend.

DE ROOS

PC Hooftstraat 183 ⓣ 020 689 0091, ⓦ roos.nl. Mon–Fri 8.30am–6pm, Sat & Sun until 5.30pm. MAP P.102, POCKET MAP B7

The downstairs café at this New Age centre on the edge of the Vondelpark is one of the most peaceful spots in the city, selling a range of drinks and organic snacks and meals. There's also a bookshop, plus yoga and meditation.

TOUSSAINT CAFÉ

Bosboom Toussaintstraat 26 ⓣ 020 685 0737, ⓦ cafe-toussaint.nl. Daily 9am–midnight. MAP P.102, POCKET MAP B5

This cosy, very friendly café, not far from the Vondelpark, makes a nice spot for lunch – excellent sandwiches, toasties, *uitsmijters* as well as a tapas-type menu, although service can be patchy.

Restaurants

CAFÉ LOETJE

Johannes Vermeerstraat 52 ⓣ 020 662 8173, ⓦ loetje.com. Daily 11am–11pm. MAP P.102, POCKET MAP C8

Excellent steaks, fries and salads are the order of the day here at this *eetcafé*. The service can be patchy, but the food is great, and inexpensive. The pleasant outdoor terrace in the summer is a bonus.

DIONYSOS

Overtoom 176 ⓣ 020 689 4441, ⓦ dionysos-taverna.nl. Tues–Sun 5.30–11pm. MAP P.102, POCKET MAP A6

This well-established and traditionally decorated Greek restaurant has the feel of a canteen, which matches the no-nonsense food and service. Covers all the classics, with a good selection of meze, plus occasional live music. Competitively priced.

GENT AAN DE SCHINKEL

Theophile de Bockstraat 1 ⓣ 020 388 2851, ⓦ gentaandeschinkel.nl. Daily 11am–1am. MAP P.102, POCKET MAP A6

Situated just outside the west end of the Vondelpark, across the pedestrian bridge, this is a lovely corner restaurant on a busy canal, serving Belgian and fusion cuisine and a huge range of bottled Belgian beers to enjoy on their summer terrace.

DE ITALIAAN

Bosboom Toussaintstraat 29 ⓣ 020 683 6854, ⓦ www.deitaliaan.com. Daily 5.30–10pm. MAP P.102, POCKET MAP B5

Dull name but the food is first-rate – Italian dishes, both a la carte and in a set menu – with mains averaging $18. The pizzas are cooked in a wood oven.

LE GARAGE

Ruysdaelstraat 54 ⓣ 020 679 7176, ⓦ restaurantlegarage.nl. Daily 6–11pm. MAP P.102 POCKET MAP C8

This elegant restaurant, with an eclectic French and Italian menu, is popular with a media crowd, since it's run by a well-known Dutch TV cook. Call to reserve at least a week in advance and dress to impress. Three-course menus are €40.

POMPA

Willemsparkweg 6 ⓣ 020 662 6206, ⓦ pompa-restaurant.nl. Daily 9am–10pm. MAP P.102, POCKET MAP B7

A bright, modern daytime café serving a good line in tapas from €6, *Pompa* morphs into a cool Italian-accented restaurant by night offering everything from classic *pasta vongole* to steak with truffle pesto. Mains average €20.

Bars

DE EBELING

Overtoom 52 ⓣ 020 777 2005, ⓦ de-ebeling.nl. Mon–Thurs & Sun 10am–3am, Fri & Sat 10am–4am. MAP P.102, POCKET MAP B6

Converted from an old bank (the toilets are in the vaults), this smart and chic lounge bar offers a good range of ales on tap and has a modern, comfortable vibe.

WILDSCHUT

Roelof Hartplein 1 ⓣ 020 676 8220, ⓦ cafewildschut.nl. Mon–Fri 9am–12.30am, Sat & Sun 10am–1am. MAP P.102, POCKET MAP C8

Not far from the Concertgebouw, this bar is famous for its Art Deco trimmings, and its large and popular pavement patio. The nicest place to drink in the area, plus a decent bar menu.

De Pijp, Nieuw Zuid and Amsterdam Oost

Amsterdam is a small city, and the majority of its residential outer districts are easily reached from the city centre. The south holds most of interest, kicking off with the vibrant De Pijp quarter, home to the Heineken Experience, and the 1930s architecture of the Nieuw Zuid (New South), which is also near the enjoyable woodland area of the Amsterdamse Bos. As for the other districts, you'll find a good deal less reason to make the effort, although the Tropenmuseum, a short walk from the Muiderpoort gate in Amsterdam East, is worth a special journey.

DE PIJP

MAP P.112, POCKET MAP D7

Across Boerenwetering, the canal to the east of the Rijksmuseum (see p.101), lies the busy heart of the Oud Zuid (Old South) – the district known as **De Pijp** ("The Pipe"), Amsterdam's first real suburb. New development beyond the Singelgracht began around 1870, but after laying down the street plans, the city council left the actual house-building to private developers. They made the most of the arrangement and constructed long rows of cheaply built and largely featureless five- and six-storey buildings, and it is these that still dominate the area today. The district's name comes from the characteristically narrow terraced streets running between long, sombre canyons of brick tenements: the apartments here were said to resemble pipe-drawers, since each had a tiny street frontage but extended deep into the building. De Pijp remains one of the city's more closely knit communities, and is home to a large proportion of new arrivals – Surinamese, Moroccan, Turkish and Asian.

Trams #16 and #24, beginning at Centraal Station, travel along the northern part of De Pijp's main drag, Ferdinand Bolstraat, as far as Albert Cuypstraat.

THE HEINEKEN EXPERIENCE

THE WETERING CIRCUIT

MAP PP.110–111, POCKET MAP D7

At the southern end of Vijzelgracht, across the Singelgracht from De Pijp, is the **Wetering circuit** roundabout, which has two low-key memorials to World War II. On the southwestern

ALBERT CUYPSTRAAT MARKET

corner of the roundabout, by the canal, is a sculpture of a wounded man holding a bugle; it was here, on March 12, 1945, that thirty people were shot by the Germans in reprisal for acts of sabotage by the Dutch Resistance – given that the war was all but over, it's hard to imagine a crueller or more futile action. Across the main street, the second memorial in the form of a brick wall commemorates H.M. van Randwijk, a Resistance leader.

HEINEKEN EXPERIENCE

Stadhouderskade 78. Tram #16, #24 from Centraal Station ⓣ 020 523 9222, ⓦ heinekenexperience.com. Sept–June Mon–Thurs 10.30am–7.30pm, Fri–Sun 10.30am–9pm; July & Aug daily 10.30am–9pm. €18, €16 if booked online. MAP P.112, POCKET MAP D7

On the northern edge of De Pijp is the former **Heineken brewery**, a whopping modern building beside the Singelgracht canal, which now holds the **Heineken Experience**. The brewery was Heineken's headquarters from 1864 to 1988, when the company was restructured and brewing was moved to a location out of town. Since then, Heineken has developed the site as a tourist attraction with lots of gimmicky but fun attractions such as virtual reality tours and displays on the history of Heineken, from advertising campaigns to beer-making. The old brewing facilities with their vast copper vats are included on the tour, but for many the main draw is the free beer you get to quaff at the end in the bar.

ALBERT CUYPMARKT

MAP P.112, POCKET MAP D7–E7

Ferdinand Bolstraat, running north–south, is De Pijp's main street, but the long east–west thoroughfare of **Albert Cuypstraat** is its heart. The general **market** here (daily except Sun 10am–5pm) – which stretches for over 1km between Ferdinand Bolstraat and Van Woustraat – is the largest in the city, with a huge array of stalls selling everything from raw-herring sandwiches to saucepans. Check out the international shops that flank the market on each side, and the good-value Indian and Surinamese restaurants down the side streets.

SARPHATIPARK

Tram #3 runs along the south side of the park, and tram #4 from Centraal Station travels along Van Woustraat, 1 block east – get off at Ceintuurbaan. MAP P.112, POCKET MAP E8

Leafy **Sarphatipark** provides a welcome splash of greenery among the surrounding brick and concrete. The park, complete with footpaths and a sinewy lake, was laid out before the construction of De Pijp got underway, and was initially intended as a place for the bourgeoisie to take a stroll.

NIEUW ZUID

MAP PP.110–111, POCKET MAP B9

Southwest of De Pijp, the **Nieuw Zuid** (New South) was the first properly planned extension to the city since the concentric canals of the seventeenth century. The Dutch architect Hendrik Petrus Berlage was responsible for the overall plan, but much of the implementation passed to a pair of prominent architects of the Amsterdam School, Michael de Klerk and Piet Kramer, and it's the playful vision of these two – turrets and bulging windows, sloping roofs and frilly balustrades – that you see in some of the buildings of the Nieuw Zuid today. These architectural peccadilloes have helped make the Nieuw Zuid one of Amsterdam's most sought-after addresses. The prime example of the area's original style is the housing estate located just north of the Amstel canal, **De Dageraad** (see opposite), while Apollolaan and Churchilllaan, are home to some of the city's most attractive - and expensive – properties. Locals pop to the shops on Beethovenstraat, the main drag running south right through the

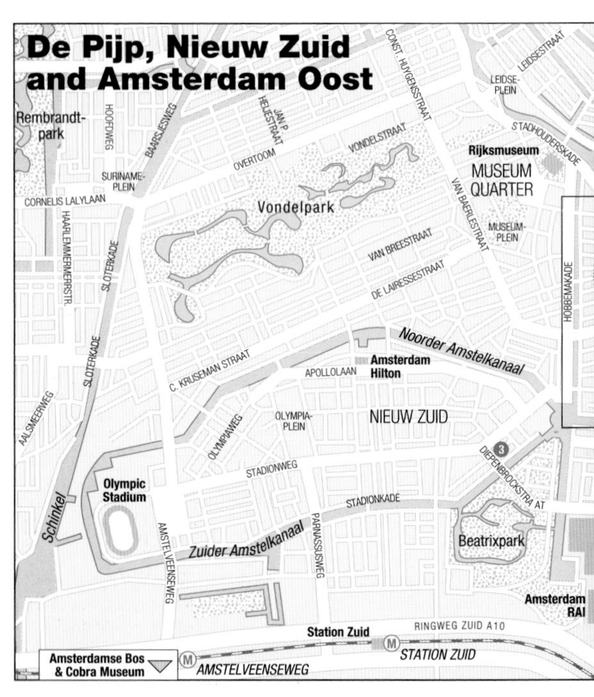

district, and stroll through the languid greenery of the Beatrixpark, whose well-tended lawns and copses are intercepted by a gentle weave of canals.

THE AMSTERDAM HILTON

Apollolaan 138. MAP PP.110–111, POCKET MAP A9

One historic footnote that might entice you this far south is the **Amsterdam Hilton**, where John Lennon and Yoko Ono staged their famous week-long "Bed-In" for peace in 1969. More recently the *Hilton* was the centre of Dutch media attention when in 2010, Herman Brood – a Dutch singer, painter and addict – committed suicide by jumping from the roof.

DE DAGERAAD

Beginning at Centraal Station, Tram #4 runs along Van Woustraat; get off at Jozef Israelskade – the Amstelkade stop – and it's a 5min walk to De Dageraad. MAP PP.110–111, POCKET MAP E9

Built between 1919 and 1922, the **De Dageraad** housing project was – indeed, is – public housing inspired by socialist utopianism, a grand vision built to elevate the working class, hence its name, "The Dawn". The handsome brick and stone work of the Berlage Lyceum marks the start of De Dageraad, with 350 workers' houses stretching beyond to either side of Pieter Lodewijk Takstraat and Burgemeester Tellegenstraat. The architects used a reinforced concrete frame as an underlay to each house, thus permitting folds, tucks and curves in the brick exteriors. Strong, angular doors, sloping roofs and turrets punctuate the facades, and you'll find a corner tower at the end of every block – it's stunning.

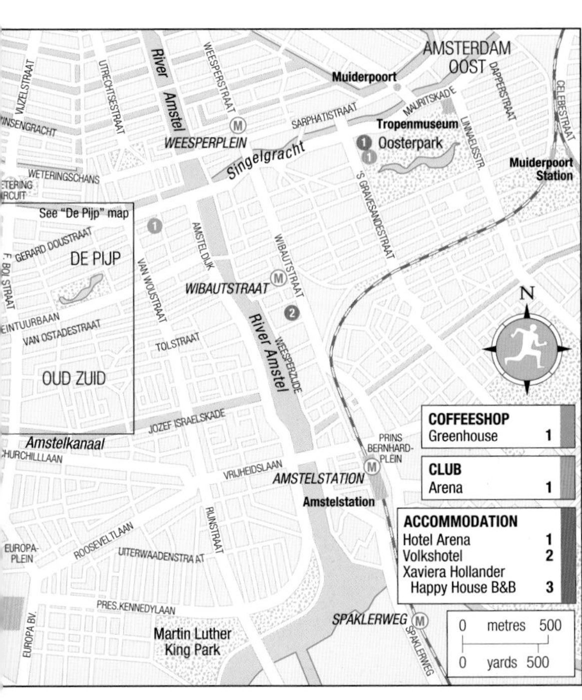

AMSTERDAMSE BOS

Main entrance at the junction of Amstelveenseweg and Van Nijenrodeweg, 3km south of the west end of the Vondelpark (see p.105). Tram #16 from Centraal Station to the Vu Medisch Centrum stop and a 400m walk amsterdamsebos.nl. MAP PP.110–111, POCKET MAP B9

With ten square kilometres of wooded parkland, the **Amsterdamse Bos** (Amsterdam Forest), to the southwest of the Nieuw Zuid, is the city's largest open space. Planted during the 1930s, the park was a large-scale attempt to provide gainful work for the city's unemployed. Originally a bleak area of flat and marshy fields, it combines a rural feel with that of a well-tended city park – and thus the "forest" tag is something of a misnomer.

In the north of the Bos, the main entrance leads to the **Bezoekerscentrum** at Bosbaanweg 5 (visitor centre; Tues–Sun 10am–5pm; free; 020 545 6100), where you can pick up maps and information, behind the centre is **Bosbaan**, a kilometre-long dead-straight canal, popular for boating and swimming, and there are children's playgrounds and spaces for various sports, including ice skating. Canoes and rowing boats can be rented just to the south of the Bosbaan, besde the Grote Vijver Lake at **Kanoverhuur Amsterdamse Bos** (April–Sept daily 10.30am–7pm; 020 645 7831), or you can simply walk or jog your way around a choice of clearly marked trails. There's bicycle rental here too, at Amsterdamse Bos Fietsverhuur, beside the path at Bosbaanweg 1 (March–Oct daily 10am–6pm; 020 644 5473).

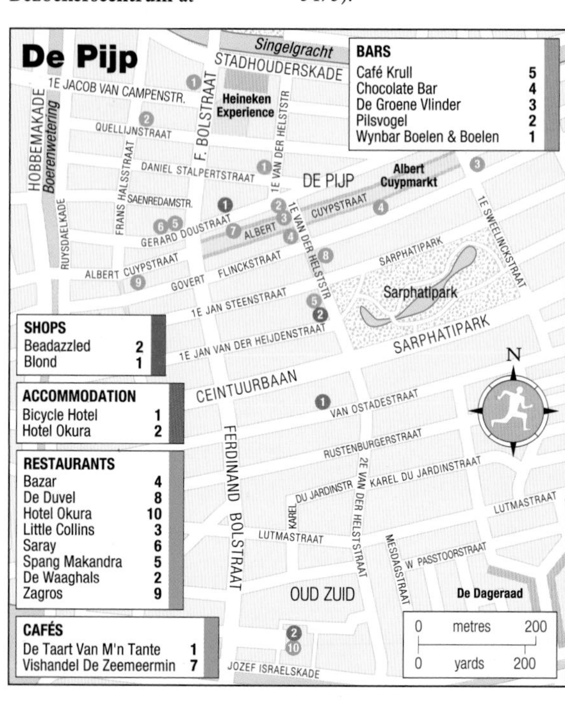

CAFÉ IN THE AMSTERDAMSE BOS

COBRA MUSEUM

Sandbergplein 1, Amstelveen. Tram #5 from Centraal Station to Amstelveen Binnehof (bus station), in front of the museum 020 547 5050, www.cobra-museum.nl. Daily 11am–5pm. €12. MAP PP.110–111, POCKET MAP B9

The **CoBrA Museum of Modern Art**, located well to the south of the Amstelveen Bos and close to the Amstelveen bus station, is soothingly white. Its glass walls give a view of the canal behind, and display the works of the artists of the CoBrA movement, which was founded in 1948. The movement grew out of artistic developments in the cities of Copenhagen, Brussels and Amsterdam – hence the name (a curled snake later became the symbol of the movement). CoBrA's first exhibition, held at Amsterdam's Stedelijk Museum, showcased the big, colourful canvases, with bold lines and confident forms, for which the movement became famous. The work displayed a spontaneity and inclusivity that was unusual for the art world of the time and it stirred a veritable hornet's nest of artistic controversy. You'll only find a scattering of the paintings in the gallery, but there's enough to get an idea of what CoBrA was about, not least in **Karel Appel**'s weird bird sculpture outside, and his brash, childlike paintings inside. Appel, along with **Constant Nieuwenhuys**, was one of the movement's leading lights. Upstairs, the museum hosts regular temporary exhibitions of works by contemporary artists. There's a good shop, too, with plenty of prints and books on CoBrA, plus a bright café where you can gaze upon Appel's sculpture at length.

THE MUIDERPOORT

South end of Plantage Middenlaan. MAP PP.110–111, POCKET MAP H6

Amsterdam East begins with Amsterdam's old eastern gate, the **Muiderpoort**, a grand Neoclassical affair through which Napoleon staged a triumphal entry into the city in 1811. The grandness of the occassion was, however, tempered by his half-starved

TROPENMUSEUM

troops, who could barely be restrained from from looting a city which was to them brimming with potential spoils.

TROPENMUSEUM

Linnaeusstraat 2. Tram #9 from Centraal Station or #14 from Dam Square ⓣ 020 568 8200, ⓦ tropenmuseum.nl. Tues–Sun 10am–5pm, also Mon during school holidays. €15, children €8. MAP PP.110–111, POCKET MAP H6

Amsterdam East's main attraction is the **Tropenmuseum**, which occupies a rambling brick building beside the Singelgracht canal. Part of the **Royal Tropical Institute**, this large ethnographic museum has room to focus on themes such as the world's cultural and historical influences, and impresses with its applied art.

One particularly interesting section is dedicated to **Dutch colonialism**, focusing on Indonesia and the Pacific. Among the many artefacts, there are Javanese stone friezes, elaborate carved wooden boats from New Guinea and, perhaps strangest of all, ritual ancestor "Bis poles" cut from giant New Guinea mangroves. The collection is imaginatively presented and there are also creative and engaging displays devoted to such subjects as music-making and puppetry. In addition there are intriguing reconstructions, down to sounds and smells, of typical settings from different countries, such as a Jamaican café or a Surinamese logger's hut.

OOSTERPARK

Tram #9 from Centraal Station runs along Linnaeusstraat on the park's eastern perimeter. MAP PP.110–111, POCKET MAP H6–H7

Next to the Tropenmuseum, the **Oosterpark** is a large slab of greenery whose mature trees, footpaths and bandstand flank a wiggly lake. It's a popular picnic spot and you can hunt out a couple of **monuments** – one to the film-maker Theo van Gogh, who was murdered in Amsterdam in 2004 (see p.145), the other the National Slavery Monument, erected in 2002 to commemorate the abolition of slavery in the Netherlands in 1863.

Shops

BEADAZZLED

Sarphatipark 6 ⓣ 020 673 4587, ⓦ www.beadazzled.nl. Mon 1–6pm, Tues–Fri 10.30am–6pm, Sat 10.30am–5pm. MAP P.112, POCKET MAP D8

Beads in all shapes and colours as well as bags, cheerfully decorated lamps and other accessories, including Havaiana flip flops for men, women and children.

BLOND

Gerard Doustraat 69 ⓣ 020 428 4929, ⓦ blond-amsterdam.nl. Mon noon–6pm, Tues–Fri 10am–6pm, Sat 10am–5pm. MAP P.112, POCKET MAP D7

Popular gift shop with hand-painted and personalized pottery, bed linen, towels and note blocks, mainly in the colour pink.

Coffeeshop

GREENHOUSE

Tolstraat 91. Tram #4 from Centraal Station to Lutmastraat stop. Daily 9am–1am. MAP PP.110–111, POCKET MAP F8

Consistently sweeps the boards at the annual Cannabis Cup, with medals for its dope as well as "Best Coffeeshop" – these guys are extremely knowledgeable in their field. Tolstraat is down to the south, but worth the trek: if you're only buying once, buy here. Also a branch nearer the centre at O.Z. Voorburgwal 191.

DE TART VAN M'N TANTE

Cafés

DE TAART VAN M'N TANTE

Ferdinand Bolstraat ⓣ 020 776 4600, ⓦ detaart.com. Daily 10am–6pm. MAP P.112, POCKET MAP D7

If there is a camper café in Amsterdam, then we have yet to find it. This pink-painted local haunt does fabulous cakes and pastries – both sweet and savoury – along with excellent tea, coffee and soft drinks.

VISHANDEL DE ZEEMEERMIN

Albert Cuypstraat 93 ⓣ 020 673 5955. Mon–Sat 9am–5pm. MAP P.112, POCKET MAP D8

What better way to round off your visit to the market than to sample the delights of this excellent – and typical – Dutch fish stall. If you're not brave enough for the raw herring there are cooked offerings too, such as calamari.

Restaurants

BAZAR

Albert Cuypstraat 182 ⓣ 020 675 0544, ⓦ bazaramsterdam.nl. Daily 11am–midnight. MAP P.112, POCKET MAP D7

This cavernous converted church is usually buzzing with activity long after the market traders have packed up. A lively place to eat dinner; choose from the Middle Eastern and North African influenced menu with tasty *mezze* and kebab.

DE DUVEL

1e van der Helststraat 59–61 020 675 7517, deduvel.nl. Daily 11am–1am, Fri & Sat till 3am. MAP P.112, POCKET MAP D8

Immensely popular *eetcafé*, always crowded, so be sure to book ahead. Toasties and sandwiches at lunchtimes; mains such as steaks, *saté* and spaghetti at dinner for €15–20. Also a popular drinking spot, especially on a warm and sunny evening when the outside pavement terrace is a fine place to be.

HOTEL OKURA

Ferdinand Bolstraat 333 020 678 7111, okura.nl. Daily 6.30–10pm. MAP P.112, POCKET MAP D9

The chi-chi *Hotel Okura* (see p.131) has four restaurants, no fewer than three of which have Michelin stars: the *Yamazato* is the finest experience of Japanese food you'll find in the city, a traditional kaiseki restaurant whose menu features expertly prepared sushi, tempura, sashimi and sukiyaki; reckon on paying upwards of €100/person. Alternatively, try the *Teppanyaki Sazanka*, a much vaunted grill restaurant, where the chef prepares fish, steaks and vegetables on a hot plate in front of you (seasonal menu €110). Booking essential.

TEPPANYAKI SAZANKA AT THE HOTEL OKURA

LITTLE COLLINS

1e Sweelinkckstraat 19 020 673 2293, littlecollins.nl. Wed 10.30am–4pm, Thurs & Fri 10.30am–10pm, Sat 9am–10pm, Sun 9am–4pm. MAP P.112, POCKET MAP E7

A little piece of Australia in Amsterdam, serving more or less anything you like – oysters, pork rillettes, Korean beef, pork belly and more. Be prepared to wait for a table.

SARAY

Gerard Doustraat 33 020 671 9216, saraylokanta.nl. Tues–Sun noon–midnight, kitchen till 10pm. MAP P.112, POCKET MAP D8

Excellent Turkish place down in the De Pijp neighbourhood. Its dark-wood, candlelit interior and living room ambience bestow an inviting backdrop for a leisurely dinner. It's cheap too, with main courses from €12.50 and a large plate of mixed *mezze* for €15.

SPANG MAKANDRA

Gerard Doustraat 39 020 670 5081, spangmakandra.nl. Mon–Sat 11am–10pm, Sun 1–10pm. MAP P.112, POCKET MAP D8

Bargain-basement Surinamese-Javanese *eetcafé*, in business since 1978. Most dishes are under €10, and you can get delicious Surinamese sandwiches for €3.50. Great flavours – and an excellent budget choice.

DE WAAGHALS

Frans Halsstraat 29 020 679 9609, waaghals.nl. Daily 5.30–10pm. MAP P.112, POCKET MAP D7

Well-prepared organic dishes in this cooperative-run restaurant near the Albert Cuyp. This place gets busy early so book ahead to be sure of a table. The menu changes twice a month, and though the food takes a while to prepare, the rewards are delicious and generously portioned. Mains around €18.

ZAGROS

Albert Cuypstraat 50 020 670 0461, www.zagrosrestaurant.nl. Tues–Sat 5–11pm. MAP P.112, POCKET MAP D8

Popular no-frills Kurdish restaurant run by four brothers. Serves traditional starters such as *tahini* and walnut salad (€5), mixed *mezze* for €14.50, and mains such as marinated lamb and chicken for €13–15.

Bars

CAFÉ KRULL

Sarphatipark 2 020 662 0214, cafekrull.com. Daily 9am–1am, Sat & Sun till 3am. MAP P.112, POCKET MAP D8

A few metres from the Albert Cuyp, this is an atmospheric and lively place. Drinks all day long, a decent light lunch menu and good music.

CHOCOLATE BAR

1e van der Helststraat 62a 020 675 7672, chocolate-bar.nl. Mon–Thurs 9am–1am, Fri & Sat 9am–3am, Sun 9am–1am. MAP P.112, POCKET MAP D8

Cool, disco-inspired café-bar that's open for tasty food – sandwiches, salads – or cocktails any time of the day. Perch at the bar on leather stools or lounge in the cosy room out the back.

DE GROENE VLINDER

Albert Cuypstraat 130 020 846 6553, cafe-de-groene-vlinder.nl. Daily 10am–1am, Fri & Sat until 3am. MAP P.112, POCKET MAP D8

Great views of the bustling market from this bright and spacious split-level café with cheap daily specials and bulky salads. The drinks menu covers all the basics.

PILSVOGEL

Gerard Douplein 14 020 664 6483, www.pilsvogel.nl. Daily 10am–1am, Fri & Sat until 3am. MAP P.112, POCKET MAP D7

Favourite drinking spot for style-conscious 30-somethings, who gather her to enjoy the laidback atmosphere and decent tapas, as well as a good selection of Spanish wines.

WYNBAR BOELEN & BOELEN

1e van der Helststraat 50 wijnbar.nl. Tues–Thurs & Sun 4pm–midnight, Fri & Sat 4pm–1am. MAP P.112, POCKET MAP D7

Tasteful wine bar close to Albert Cuypstraat market with a huge selection of wines. A heated terrace provides alfresco eating even in the cooler months, and the French-inspired menu offers seafood delights such as a half-dozen oysters for €20.

Club

ARENA

's-Gravensandestraat 51. Metro to Weesperplein, then an 8min walk 020 850 2400, www.hotelarena.nl. Fri & Sat 10/11pm–4am. MAP PP.110–111, POCKET MAP H6

Hip club set in a restored chapel adjoining a deluxe hotel that used to be an orphanage and an asylum. Open Fridays and Saturdays, with occasional special events. International DJs sometimes drop by – and there's a delightful cocktail lounge here too (daily noon–2am).

Day-trips from Amsterdam

Amsterdammers may well tell you that there's nothing remotely worth seeing outside their own city, but the fact is you're spoilt for choice, with fast and efficient rail connections putting about a third of the country within easy reach of a day-trip. There are any number of places you can get to, including most of the towns of the Randstaad conurbation that stretches south and east of Amsterdam and encompasses the country's other big cities, The Hague, Utrecht and Rotterdam, but we've picked a few of the closer highlights. The easiest trip you could make is to Haarlem, just fifteen minutes away by train, a pleasant provincial town that is home to the outstanding Frans Hals Museum. There's also the showcase of the country's flower growers, the Keukenhof Gardens, worth visiting in spring and summer, while to the north of Amsterdam the most obvious targets are Volendam and Marken, two old seaports bordering the freshwater IJsselmeer and Markermeer lakes, formerly – before the enclosing dykes were put in – the saltwater Zuider Zee. No trains venture out along this part of the coast, but it's an easy bus ride from Amsterdam, also taking in the beguiling one-time shipbuilding centre of Edam, which is, of course, famous for its cheese. A little further afield – and this time on the train network – is the charming seaport of Enkhuizen.

HAARLEM

HAARLEM

An easy fifteen-minute train journey (6 hourly) from Amsterdam's Centraal Station, **Haarlem** has a very different feel from its big-city neighbour. Once a flourishing cloth-making centre, the town avoided the worst excesses of industrialization and nowadays it's an easily absorbed place with an attractive centre studded with fine old buildings. The **Grote Kerk** (bavo.nl; Mon–Sat 10am–5pm; €2.50), right in the centre of town on the Grote Markt, is well worth seeing, a soaring Gothic church with a magnificent eighteenth-century organ. But the real draw is the outstanding **Frans Hals Museum**, located in the Oudemannhuis, or almshouse, where the artist spent his last and, for some, his most brilliant years. Located at Groot Heiligland 62 (Tues–Sat 11am–5pm, Sun noon–5pm; €12.50; 023 511 5775, franshalsmuseum.nl), the museum is a five-minute stroll south from the Grote Markt – take pedestrianized Warmoesstraat and then Schagchelstraat and keep straight ahead.

The museum has a number of works by Haarlem painters other than Hals, with canvases by Jan van Scorel, Karel van Mander and Cornelis Cornelisz van Haarlem. Chief among the paintings by Hals himself is the set of "Civic Guard" portraits with which he made his name. Displayed together, these make a powerful impression, alongside the artist's later, darker works, the most notable of which are the twin Regents and Regentesses of the Oudemannenhuis itself.

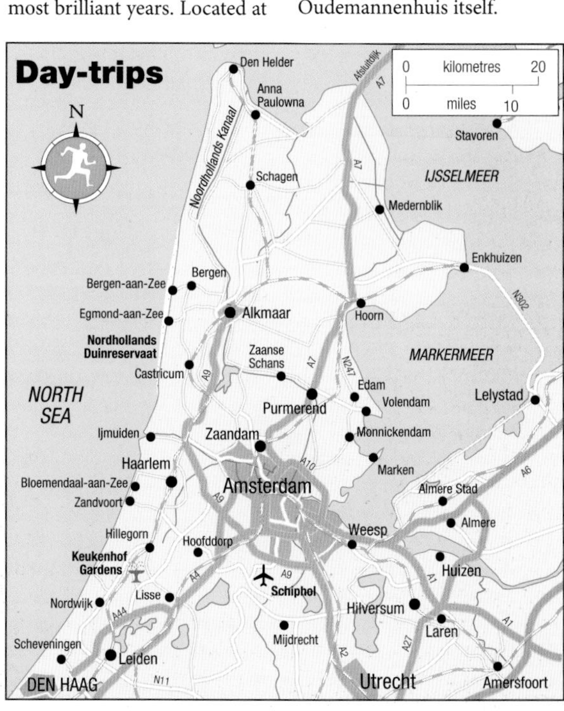

KEUKENHOF GARDENS

Stationsweg 166, Lisse 025 246 5555, keukenhof.nl. Late March to late May daily 8am–7.30pm. €16.

The pancake-flat fields extending south from Haarlem towards Leiden are the heart of the **Dutch bulbfields**, whose bulbs and blooms support a billion-dollar industry and some ten-thousand growers, as well as attracting tourists in droves. The small town of **Lisse**, halfway between Leiden and Haarlem, is home to the showcase **Keukenhof Gardens**, the largest flower gardens in the world. The site is the former estate of a fifteenth-century countess, who used to grow herbs and vegetables for her dining table, hence "Keukenhof", which means "kitchen garden". Some seven million flowers are on show for their full flowering period, complemented, in case of especially harsh winters, by 5000 square metres of glasshouses holding indoor displays. You could easily spend a whole day here, swooning among the sheer abundance of it all, but to get the best of it you need to come early, before the tour buses pack the place. There are several restaurants in the extensive grounds, and well-marked paths take you all the way through the gardens, which specialize in daffodils, hyacinths and, of course, tulips.

To get to the Keukenhof by public transport from Amsterdam, take the train to Leiden or Centraal Station (every 30min; 40min), then catch Arriva Keukenhof Express bus #854 (every 15min; 30min) from the adjacent bus station.

VOLENDAM

The former fishing village of **Volendam** is the largest of the towns bordering the Markermeer and was once something of an artists' retreat, visited by Renoir and Picasso and always a favoured location for local painters. The **Volendams Museum**, on the edge of the town centre at Zeestraat 41 (029 936 9258, volendamsmuseum.nl; mid-March–Oct daily 10am–5pm; €3) has lots of local work on display, not least a series of mosaics made up of eleven million cigar bands, the work of an eccentric local artist. It's also worth popping into the waterfront *Hotel*

THE KEUKENHOF GARDENS

Spaander, where the public rooms are decorated with paintings and sketches given to the hotel by impoverished artists in lieu of rent.

Volendam is reachable from the bus station at the back of Amsterdam Centraal by EBS bus #316 (every 30min; 30min; Ⓦ localbus.nl); get off on Julianaweg, about 400m from the waterfront along Zeestraat. The bus also runs to Edam (10min), and although there are no buses from Volendam to Marken, there is a passenger ferry (March–Oct daily 10am–6pm, every 30min–1hr; Nov–Feb limited service; 25min; Ⓦ markenexpress.nl; €7.50 one way, €10 return).

MARKEN HOUSE

MARKEN

The tiny island of **Marken** was pretty much a closed community, supported by a small fishing industry, until its road connection to the mainland was completed in 1957. Nowadays, the fishing has all but disappeared, though the island – or rather its one and only village, Marken – retains a picturesque charm of immaculately maintained green wooden houses, clustered on top of mounds first raised to protect the islanders from the sea. There are two main parts to the village: waterfront Havenbuurt, which is dotted with souvenir shops, often staffed by locals in traditional costume; and the quieter Kerkbuurt, centred on the church, whose narrow lanes are lined by ancient dwellings and one-time eel-smoking houses.

You can take a passenger ferry to Marken from Volendam (see above); or you can get there direct from the bus station at the back of Amsterdam Centraal on EBS bus #315 (every 30min; 40min; Ⓦ localbus.nl). In Marken, passengers are dropped off beside the car park on the edge of the village, from where it's a five-minute walk to the waterfront. Note that there are no buses from Marken to Edam or Volendam.

EDAM

Considering the international fame of the red balls of cheese that carry its name, you might expect the village of **Edam**, just 12km or so up along the coast from Marken, to be jam-packed with tourists. In fact, Edam usually lacks the crowds of its island neighbour and remains a delightful, good-looking and prosperous little town of neat brick houses and slender canals. Nowadays, the one real crowd puller is Edam's **cheese market**, held every Wednesday morning from July to mid-August on the Kaasmarkt (10.30am–12.30pm), but the real pleasure is in wandering its charming streets and canals, and maybe renting a bike to cycle down to the Markemeer lake. Bike rental is available at Ronald Schot, Grote Kerkstraat 7 (029 937 2155, www.ronaldschot.nl). EBS bus #316 (every 30min; 40min; localbus.nl), links the bus station at the back of Amsterdam Centraal with Edam's bus station on the southwest edge of town, on Singelweg, a 5–10-minute walk from the centre. The bus also goes to Volendam, 3km away (10min). Note that there are no buses from Edam to Marken.

ENKHUIZEN

Nudging up against the waters of the IJsselmeer, **Enkhuizen** (trains from Amsterdam Centraal every 30min; 1hr) was once one of the country's most important seaports. Nowadays, things are much quieter, but the town centre, with its ancient streets, slender canals and pretty harbours, is wonderfully well preserved, a rough circle with a ring of bastions and moat on one side, and the old sea dyke on the other. A good place to start an exploration is the Oude Haven, which stretches east in a gentle curve to the conspicuous **Drommedaris**, a heavy-duty brick watchtower built in 1540 to guard the harbour entrance. Beyond the Drommedaris is the picturesque **Buitenhaven**, with its sailing boats and barges, and beyond, on Wierdijk, is the town's star turn, the excellent **Zuiderzeemuseum**, which divides into two – an indoor section (daily 10am–5pm; combined entrance €16; 022 835 1111, zuiderzeemuseum.nl) of around a dozen rooms devoted to annual exhibitions on different aspects of the Zuider Zee, and an outdoor section, the Museumpark (April to late Oct daily 10am–5pm), which comprises a collection of original buildings moved here over the last decades. Highlights of the indoor section are concentrated in the impressive ship hall, where you can get up close and personal with a number of traditional sailing barges and other craft, for example a dinghy for duck-hunting, complete with shotgun. In the Museumpark, there are vintage stores, workshops and even streets that have been transported here from every part of the region, and which together provide the flavour of life hereabouts from 1880 to around 1932. Just about everything is worth seeing, but high points include a reconstruction of Marken harbour as of 1900, old fishermen's houses from Urk, a post office and a pharmacy that has a marvellous collection of "gapers" – painted wooden heads with their tongues out, which were the traditional sign of a pharmacist. The museum strives to be authentic: sheep and goats roam the surrounding meadows, its smokehouses smoke (and sell) herring and eels, and the sweetshop sells real old-fashioned sweets.

ENKHUIZEN

Bars and restaurants

DAMHOTEL

Keizersgracht 1, Edam ⓣ 029 937 1766, ⓦ damhotel.nl. Daily noon–10pm.

The bar here is a cosy place for a drink, and it has a decent lunch menu of sandwiches, salads and pancakes for €5–20 and light mains for €16–20. Plus the hotel has the upmarket but excellent-value *Auberge* restaurant, which serves an ambitious menu of starters for €10–12 and rich and enticing mains for around €25.

DIE DRIE HARINGHE

Dijk 28, Enkhuizen ⓣ 022 831 8610, ⓦ drieharinghe.nl. Wed–Sun 5–10pm.

Housed in an immaculately renovated seventeenth-century building down on the harbour, with tables in the courtyard garden outside and by the canal, this is Enkhuizen's best restaurant, with a menu that's strong on seafood and local specialities. Mains are around €25. Reservations advised.

HOTEL SPAANDER

Haven 15–19, Volendam ⓣ 029 936 3595, ⓦ hotelspaander.nl. Daily noon–9.30pm.

This creaky old hotel right on the waterfront in Volendam is very much the town's hub, with a nice bar for a drink or a coffee and a good brasserie serving lots of fishy specialities for lunch and dinner. Mains from $21.

JACOBUS PIECK

Warmoesstraat 18, Haarlem ⓣ 023 532 6144, ⓦ jacobuspieck.nl. Tues–Sat 11am–4pm & 5.30–10pm.

Welcoming place that's a good bet for both lunch and dinner, with burgers and salads during the day and a Mediterranean-inspired menu in the evening with main courses for around €18. There's a secluded garden too.

DE JOPENKERK

Gedempte Voldersgracht 2, Haarlem ⓣ 023 533 4114, ⓦ jopenkerk.nl. Daily 10am–1am, lunch noon–3pm, dinner 5.30–9pm.

This converted old church is a microbrewery bar and restaurant rolled into one, with long benches, comfy sofas and its own cloudy, unfiltered beer. The food is simple rather than splendid, but you should at least try one of the dozen or so Jopen brews at the bar.

LAND EN ZEEZICHT

Havenbuurt 6, Marken ⓣ 029 960 1302. Daily 11am–8.30pm.

More of a lunch than dinner spot, but very cosy, overlooking the harbour and serving a mean smoked-eel sandwich.

DE SMEDERIJ

Breedstraat 158–160, Enkhuizen ⓣ 022 831 4604, ⓦ restaurantdesmederij.nl. May–Sept Mon, Tues & Thurs–Sun 5–10pm; Oct–April Mon, Tues & Fri–Sun 5–10pm.

Inventive, French-Mediterranean cuisine in a smartly renovated building a block back from the harbour, with starters for €12, main courses for around €25.

STEMPELS

Klokhuisplein 9, Haarlem ⓣ 023 512 3910, ⓦ stempelsinhaarlem.nl. Daily: brasserie 8am–10pm, restaurant 5.30–10pm.

Haarlem's best brasserie and restaurant serves up great fish and meat dishes prepared in innovative ways – try, for example, the grilled bass with tomato risotto and anchovies. Mains in the restaurant start at around €25, or you'll spend about €14 for the simpler dishes in the brasserie.

AMSTERDAM

ACCOMMODATION

Hotels

Despite a slew of new hotels, from chic designer places through to chain high-rises, hotel accommodation in Amsterdam can still be difficult to find and is, more often than not, a major expense. Indeed, such is the city's popularity as a short-break destination that advance reservations are pretty much essential at any time of the year, though there tends to be more slack on Sunday and Monday nights. Prices fluctuate wildly with demand, so the rates we quote should serve only as a broad guideline. Prices are usually more affordable further from the centre – a standard-issue double room in the Grachtengordel can, for example, cost twice as much as a comparable room in the suburbs.

The Old Centre

THE EXCHANGE > Damrak 50 T 020 523 0080, W www.hoteltheexchange.com. MAP PP.34–35, POCKET MAP B11. God knows, Damrak needs a decent hotel, and this sister to the excellent *Lloyd Hotel* (see p.130) is a welcome and wacky addition, with the same range of budget to luxury rooms, each eccentrically designed by students of the Amsterdam Fashion Institute. Full of cool character, and for the price one of the best places to sleep in town. There's also a sleek downstairs café, *Stock*. **€130**

HOTEL DE L'EUROPE > Nieuwe Doelenstraat 2–8 T 020 531 1777, W leurope.nl. MAP PP.34–35, POCKET MAP B14. One of the city's top hotels, and retaining a wonderful fin-de-siecle charm, with large, well-furnished rooms, an attractive riverside terrace and a great central location. A canal view will cost you another €50 or so, but this is about as luxurious as the city gets. Breakfast not included. **€330**

LE COIN > Nieuwe Doelenstraat 5 T 020 524 6800, W lecoin.nl. MAP PP.34–35, POCKET MAP B14. In a good location opposite the swanky *Hotel de l'Europe*, but a quarter of the price. All rooms have kitchenettes and are kitted out in contemporary fashion. **€140**

MISC > Kloveniersburgwal 20 T 020 330 6241, W misceatdrinksleep.com. MAP PP.34–35, POCKET MAP C12. Excellent, very friendly independent hotel on the edge of the Red Light District, with six good-sized rooms each with a different theme. Breakfast included. **€225**

NES > Kloveniersburgwal 137–139 T 020 624 4773, W hotelnes.nl. MAP PP.34–35, POCKET MAP C14. A pleasant and quiet hotel with helpful staff, well positioned away from noise, but still close to shops and nightlife. The size of the functional rooms can vary quite a bit, so don't be afraid to ask to see other rooms if yours looks on the small side. **€150**

NH CITY CENTRE > Spuistraat 288 T 020 420 4545, W nh-hotels.com. MAP PP.34–35, POCKET MAP A13. A chain hotel, but an appealing one, in a sympathetically renovated 1920s Art Deco former textile factory, and well situated for the cafés and bars of the Spui and around. Some of the rooms have canal views, and all boast extremely comfy beds and good showers. Breakfast included. **€180**

NH GRAND HOTEL KRASNAPOLSKY > Dam 9 T 020 554 9111, W nh-hotels.com. MAP PP.34–35, POCKET MAP B12. Located in a huge and striking mid-nineteenth-century

Prices and tax

The least expensive hotels charge around €120 for a double room, a little less if you share a bathroom, but don't expect too much in the way of creature comforts at these sort of prices – you only really hit any sort of comfort zone at about €150. Breakfast – bread, jam, eggs, ham and cheese – is usually included in the price of a room, but at budget and moderately priced hotels, it's often extra. One other thing to bear in mind: some of the cheaper hotels request full payment in advance or on arrival.

building, this five-star hotel occupies virtually an entire side of Dam Square. Its rooms are nicely done, if unspectacular. Bargains are sometimes available. **€240**

PARK PLAZA VICTORIA > Damrak 1–5 **T 020 623 4255, W parkplaza.com.** MAP PP.34–35, POCKET MAP C11. This tall, elegant building opposite Centraal Station is geared towards business travellers and split into two sections: the 306-room Victoria Wing, with rooms suited to the classical style of the old building; and the new 164-room Urban Wing, whose rooms have a more modern, fashionable edge. Amenities include a lounge bar with occasional live jazz, restaurant, fitness centre and pool. It's pricey, but there are often bargains to be had. **€250**

SINT NICOLAAS > Spuistraat 1a **T 020 626 1384, W hotelnicolaas.nl.** MAP PP.34–35, POCKET MAP B11. Quirkier than many of the other three-star hotels in the area, the St Nicolaas's cosy downstairs bar-reception gives way to 27 comfortable refurbished rooms, all with baths. Conveniently located too, just five minutes' walk from Centraal Station. **€230**

WINSTON > Warmoesstraat 129 **T 020 623 1380, W winston.nl.** MAP PP.34–35, POCKET MAP C12. Part of the St Christopher's Inns chain, this self-consciously young and cool hotel-cum-hostel has funky rooms decorated with crazy art, and a busy ground-floor bar that has regular live music. It's a formula that works a treat; the *Winston* is often full – though this is probably also due to its low prices which include breakfast. Dorm beds available too, from around €35 a head during high season. Lift and full disabled access. Ten minutes' walk from Centraal Station. **€110**

The Grachtengordel

AMBASSADE > Herengracht 341 **T 020 555 0222, W ambassade-hotel.nl.** MAP PP.54–55, POCKET MAP A13. Elegant canalside hotel made up of ten seventeenth-century houses with smartly furnished lounges, a well-stocked library and comfortable en-suite rooms, decorated in period-meets-countryhouse style. **€250**

AMSTERDAM AMERICAN > Leidsekade 97 **T 020 556 3000, W hampshirehotels.com.** MAP PP.54–55, POCKET MAP B6. Landmark Art Deco hotel just off Leidseplein that dates from 1900, though the bedrooms themselves are mostly kitted out in standard modern style. Large, double-glazed doubles. **€220**

BACKSTAGE HOTEL > Leidsegracht 114 **T 020 624 4044, W backstagehotel.com.** MAP PP.54–55, POCKET MAP B5. This hotel is aimed at musicians playing at the nearby *Melkweg* and *Paradiso*, and furnishings like theatre mirrors, spotlights and flight cases in the 22 rooms are designed to make them feel at home. Everyone can enjoy the free internet, 24hr bar and pool table. **€145**

CHIC & BASIC > Herengracht 13 **T 020 522 2345, W chicandbasic.com.** MAP PP.54–55, POCKET MAP B10. Dutch branch of this spunky Spanish concept, with 26 basic but

Booking hotels

You can obviously book direct online or by phone, or you can compare prices and availability through the usual accommodation booking engines. Once you've arrived, the city's tourist offices (see p.141) will make on-the-spot hotel reservations on your behalf for a small fee, but during peak periods and weekends they get extremely busy with long and time-consuming queues. The good news is that the city's compactness means that you'll almost inevitably end up somewhere central.

cool rooms, some overlooking the canal. The changeable lighting allows you to adjust the colour of your room according to your mood – a cheapo gimmick, but an effective one. Breakfast not included. **€180**

CLEMENS > **Raadhuisstraat 39 020 624 6089, clemenshotel .nl.** MAP PP.54–55, POCKET MAP C3. Well-run budget hotel in a good location close to the Anne Frank Huis, and one of the better options along this busy main road. All rooms have wi-fi, flatscreen TVs and a/c. Doubles with shower are more expensive. **€150**

DIKKER & THIJS FENICE > **Prinsengracht 444 020 620 1212, dikkerandthijshotelamsterdam .com.** MAP PP.54–55, POCKET MAP C5. Small and stylish hotel not far from Leidseplein. Rooms vary in decor but all include a minibar, telephone and TV. Those on the top floor have good views of the city. **€180**

DYLAN > **Keizersgracht 384 020 530 2010, dylanamsterdam.com.** MAP PP.54–55, POCKET MAP C4. One of Amsterdam's smartest hotels, housed in a seventeenth-century building that centres on a beautiful courtyard and terrace. Boutique in size and style, its forty sumptuous rooms range from opulent reds or greens to minimal white decor. The Michelin-starred restaurant offers French cuisine and the bar is open to non-guests. **€450**

ESTHEREA > **Singel 303–309 020 624 5146, estherea.nl.** MAP PP.54–55, POCKET MAP A13. Comfortable four-star converted from a couple of sympathetically modernized canal houses. There's no hankering after minimalism here, with thick, plush carpets and beds that you literally sink into. **€250**

HEGRA > **Herengracht 269 020 623 7877, hotelhegra.nl.** MAP PP.54–55, POCKET MAP A13. This family-run hotel has a welcoming atmosphere and is pretty good value considering the location, on a handsome stretch of canal near the Spui. Recently refurbished rooms are small but comfortable. Breakfast included. **€145**

'T HOTEL > **Leliegracht 18 020 422 2741, thotel.nl.** MAP PP.54–55, POCKET MAP A11. Appealing hotel located in an old high-gabled house along a quiet stretch of canal. The eight spacious rooms are decorated in bright, modern style with large beds and either bath or shower. No groups. Minimum three-night stay at the weekend; includes breakfast. **€170**

THE HOXTON > **Herengracht 255 020 888 5555, thehoxton.com /amsterdam.** MAP PP.54–55, POCKET MAP A12 This outstanding hotel, the first opening outside London of this über-cool mini-chain, occupies five conjoined seventeenth-century canal houses. The interior is a sight to behold, the public rooms an exercise in exquisite Modernist taste, all clean lines with splashes of colour. The guest rooms, all 111 of them, are similarly tasteful ranging from the snug ("Cosy") to the more spacious ("Roomy"). Tram #1, #2 or #5 to the Dam. **€250**

HOTEL 717 > **Prinsengracht 717 020 427 0717, www.717hotel.nl.** MAP PP.54–55, POCKET MAP C5. Deluxe canal house hotel with just nine suites, all individually designed. Great, large spaces, beautifully conceived, and one of the most luxurious small hotels in the city. **€275**

MAISON RIKA > Oude Spiegelstraat 12 ⓣ 020 330 1112, ⓦ rikaint.com. Tram #1, #2 or #5 to Spui. MAP PP.54–55, POCKET MAP A13. Housed in a former art gallery, this self-styled boutique hotel has two beautifully furnished queen-sized bedrooms on the second and third floors and is owned by a local fashion designer. There's free water, chocolates, tea and coffee, but no breakfast. **€250**

MARCEL'S CREATIVE EXCHANGE > Leidsestraat 87 ⓣ 020 622 9834, ⓦ marcelamsterdam.nl. MAP PP.54–55, POCKET MAP C5. Popular B&B run by an English-speaking graphic designer and artist who attracts like-minded people to this stylishly restored house with a choice of en-suite doubles, a suite and separate apartments. Decor is chic and comfortable. Relaxing and peaceful amid the buzz of the city. You'll need to book well in advance in high season. Breakfast isn't included, but there are tea- and coffee-making facilities. **€160**

PRINSENHOF > Prinsengracht 810 ⓣ 020 623 1772, ⓦ hotelprinsenhof .com. MAP PP.54–55, POCKET MAP E6. Tastefully decorated, this is one of the city's top budget options. Booking essential. Tram #4 from Centraal Station to Prinsengracht. Cheaper rooms without shower. **€100**

SEVEN BRIDGES > Reguliersgracht 31 ⓣ 020 623 1329, ⓦ sevenbridgeshotel.nl. MAP PP.54–55, POCKET MAP E5. Very charming place – and excellent value for money. It takes its name from its canalside location, which affords a view of seven dinky little bridges. Beautifully decorated in an antique style, its spotless rooms are regularly revamped. Small and popular, so reservations are pretty much essential. Breakfast is included in the price and served in your room. Trams #16, #24 or #25 from Centraal Station to Keizersgracht. **€120**

SINGEL HOTEL > Singel 13–17 ⓣ 020 626 3108, ⓦ singelhotel.nl. MAP PP.54–55, POCKET MAP B10. Pleasant hotel located in three charming canal houses right next to the old Lutheran church, a 5min walk from Centraal Station. The rooms are rather small and functional, but well equipped, and some overlook the Singel canal. **€140**

THE TIMES HOTEL > Herengracht 135 ⓣ 020 330 6030, ⓦ thetimeshotel .nl. MAP PP.54–55, POCKET MAP A11. Colourful designer hotel with a wink to the old Dutch masters – it's decked out with reproductions of paintings by Rembrandt, Vermeer et al in every room. Good location, and free wi-fi. Excludes breakfast. **€159**

TOREN > Keizersgracht 164 ⓣ 020 622 6352, ⓦ thetoren.nl. MAP PP.54–55, POCKET MAP C3. Retro-chic boutique hotel, converted from two elegant canal houses. All rooms have been renovated, some have large jacuzzis and there's also an annexe. There's a sumptuous bar/ breakfast room downstairs. **€270**

WALDORF ASTORIA > Herengracht 542–556 ⓣ 020 718 4600, ⓦ waldorfastoria3.hilton.com. MAP PP.54–55, POCKET MAP E5. As the address suggests, this is a conversion of several of Herengracht's most elegant canal houses and is as comfy a place to stay as you could wish for, with 93 spacious rooms furnished in contemporary style in a great location just south of Rembrandtplein. The loft rooms especially are lovely. **€600**

WEBER > Marnixstraat 397 ⓣ 020 627 2327, ⓦ hotelweber.nl. MAP PP.54–55, POCKET MAP B5. Seven spacious studio apartments decorated in a brisk, modern style above a popular bar, mainly attracting a youthful clientele. Small in-room breakfast provided. **€140**

WIECHMANN > Prinsengracht 328–332 ⓣ 020 626 3321, ⓦ hotelwiechmann.nl. MAP PP.54–55, POCKET MAP C4. Family-run for over fifty years, this hotel occupies an attractively restored canal house close to the Anne Frank Huis, with dark wooden beams and restrained style throughout. Large, bright rooms are in good condition with TV and shower. **€140**

The Jordaan and western docklands

LINDEN > Lindengracht 251 ⓣ 020 622 1460, ⓦ lindenhotel.nl. Take bus #18 to Willemstraat, or a 15min walk from Centraal Station. MAP P.73, POCKET MAP B2. This medium-sized hotel, in the heart of the Jordaan, is on a corner, so some of the rooms have good views. The guest rooms, which sleep two to four people, are rather nondescript, with small beds and a shower room, but perfectly adequate. **€155**

The eastern docklands and Amsterdam Noord

CRANE HOTEL FARALDA > NDSM-Plein 78 ⓣ 020 760 6161, ⓦ faralda.com. MAP P.95, POCKET MAP E1. Probably the world's first hotel in a crane offers three ultra-contemporary suites with knee-buckling city views. Bungee jumping from the top costs €85 a go, or there's the more relaxing spa pool. As you'd expect, there's a long waiting list, so book well in advance. A 10min ferry ride from Centraal Station. **€450**

LLOYD HOTEL > Oostelijke Handelskade 34 ⓣ 020 561 3607, ⓦ lloydhotel.com. MAP PP.92–93, POCKET MAP H3. Situated in the up-and-coming Oosterdok district, this former workers' hostel has been renovated to become one of Amsterdam's coolest hotels. Rather pretentiously subtitled a "cultural embassy" (it has an arts centre and library), the rooms range from one-star affairs to five-star offerings. Some rooms are great, others not so – don't be afraid to ask to change. The location is better than you might think – just five minutes' by tram #26 from Centraal Station. One-star **€90**, five-star, **€170**

The Museum Quarter and around

BILDERBERG HOTEL JAN LUYKEN > Jan Luykenstraat 58 ⓣ 020 573 0730, ⓦ bilderberg.nl. MAP P.102, POCKET MAP B6. Good-sized, nicely refurbished rooms mark out this decent stab at a mini four-star, full-service hotel. There's wi-fi in rooms, 24hr room service and a nice lounge and bar too. **€170**

COLLEGE > Roelof Hartstraat 1 ⓣ 020 571 1511, ⓦ thecollegehotel.com. MAP P.102, POCKET MAP C8. Converted from an old schoolhouse, the *College* is one of the most elegant and original additions to Amsterdam's hotel scene. Original because it's largely run by students from the city's catering school; elegant because of the sheer class of the refurbishment. **€175**

CONSCIOUS HOTEL MUSEUM SQUARE > De Lairessestraat 7 ⓣ 020 671 9596, ⓦ conscioushotels.com. MAP P.102, POCKET MAP B8. This hotel is proud of being one hundred percent sustainable, from the living plant wall by reception to the 36 rooms, which feature photographic forest wallpaper, desks made out of recycled yoghurt pots, and ergonomic beds. Other pluses are the scrumptious organic breakfast, bike rental and hotel garden. Tram #16 to Jacob Obrechtstraat. **€140**

CONSERVATORIUM > Van Baerlestraat 27 ⓣ 020 570 0000, ⓦ conservatoriumhotel.com. MAP P.102, POCKET MAP B7. Arguably the city's most jaw-dropping hotel, this heritage building – once a Conservatorium – has been transformed into a contemporary design wonderland. Standard guestrooms come with access to Akasha – the city's largest and most opulent spa. Tram #5 to Van Baerlestraat. **€450**

JL 76 > Jan Luikenstraat 76 ⓣ 020 515 0453, ⓦ hoteljlno76 .com. MAP P.102, POCKET MAP B7. Just five minutes' around the corner from its sister hotel the *Vondel* (see p.131), this is the latest in a chic mini-chain, with the same contemporary vibe and high standards. Rooms are cool, sleek and simple, with iPod docking stations, coffee machines and DVD players – and, hey, you can even watch TV in the bath. There's free wi-fi throughout, and a pleasant lounge downstairs with an honesty bar and iPad for customer use. **€180**

PIET HEIN > Vossiusstraat 51–53 ⓣ 020 662 7205, ⓦ www.hotelpiethein.nl. MAP P.102, POCKET MAP B6. Five minutes' walk from Leidseplein, the best rooms at this three-star have views over the entrance to the Vondelpark or are in the modern annexe overlooking its peaceful back garden (these are slightly more expensive). There's also a comfy bar that's open till 1am. Lift access. **€180**

ROEMER > Roemer Visscherstraat 10 ⓣ 020 589 0800, ⓦ hotelroemer.com. MAP P.102, POCKET MAP B6. Four-star hotel in an extensively revamped old house and with a pleasant garden out the back. Rooms vary considerably in terms of both comfort and aesthetics. **€189**

VONDEL > Vondelstraat 26 ⓣ 020 612 0120, ⓦ hotelvondel.com. MAP P.102, POCKET MAP B6. Part of a small chain of design-conscious boutique hotels, this place is as cool as its cousins, with black paint and light natural wood characterizing the guest rooms. There's a pleasant bar and breakfast room and modern art decorates the walls of the common areas. Doubles vary in size. **€160**

De Pijp, Nieuw Zuid and Amsterdam Oost

BICYCLE HOTEL > Van Ostadestraat 123 ⓣ 020 679 3452, ⓦ bicyclehotel.com. MAP P.112, POCKET MAP D8. Friendly place down a quiet residential street, not far from Albert Cuyp market in De Pijp. It bills itself as the "bicycle hotel", renting bikes for €7.50 per day and giving advice on routes and suchlike. Garage parking available, though you'll need to book in advance. Basic but clean en-suite two-, three- and four-bed rooms, with cheaper rates for shared facilities. Tram #25 from Centraal Station to 1e van de Helststraat. Breakfast included. **€120**

HOTEL ARENA > 's-Gravesandestraat 51 ⓣ 020 850 2400, ⓦ www.hotelarena.nl. MAP PP.110–111, POCKET MAP H6. A little way east of the centre, in a renovated old orphanage on the edge of the Oosterpark, this place has been thoroughly revamped, transforming a popular hostel into a hip three-star hotel complete with split-level rooms and minimalist decor. Despite the odd pretentious flourish, it manages to retain a relaxed vibe attracting both businesspeople and travellers alike. Lively bar, intimate restaurant, and late-night club (Fri & Sat) located within the former chapel. **€129**

HOTEL OKURA > Ferdinand Bolstraat 333 ⓣ 020 678 7111, ⓦ okura.nl. MAP P.112, POCKET MAP D9. Don't be fooled by the concrete, purpose-built facade: this deluxe five-star hotel comes equipped with all the luxuries you would expect, such as a health club and sauna, and even a shopping arcade. Rooms have huge marble bathrooms, and, in the suites, mood lighting and control units for the curtains. Two of its four restaurants have Michelin stars. If you're feeling flush you could book "The Suite", set over two floors with a suspended glass staircase, private butler and cinema; a night here will set you back €12,500. **€250**

VOLKSHOTEL > Wibautstraat 150 ⓣ 020 261 2100, ⓦ volkshotel.nl. MAP PP.110–111, POCKET MAP G8. Opened in the summer of 2014 in the former offices of the Dutch newspaper *De Volkskrant*, this place really does do what it says on the tin, with cheap rates and great views from most of its 172 rooms, which were designed according to nine different, somewhat wacko concepts. Other perks include a rooftop sauna and hot tub. **€90**

XAVIERA HOLLANDER HAPPY HOUSE B&B > Stadionweg 17 ⓣ 020 673 3934, ⓦ xavierahollander.com. MAP P.110–111, POCKET MAP B9. A bit out of the way in the chi-chi Nieuw Zuid, but this B&B, run by Xaviera Hollander, one of the city's most famous former madams and author of *The Happy Hooker*, is a real Amsterdam experience, with a couple of kitschy rooms kitted out in bright colours plus the odd semi-clad female photo. Both rooms have shared facilities, but it's still very comfortable and welcoming. **€130**

Hostels

The least expensive central option is to take a dorm bed in a hostel – and there are plenty to choose from: Hostelling International places, unofficial private hostels, even Christian hostels. Most hostels will either provide (relatively) clean bed linen or charge a few euros for it – frankly your own sleeping bag might be a better option. Many hostels also lock guests out for a short period each day to clean the place, and some set a nightly curfew, though these are usually late enough not to cause too much of a problem. Note that many hostels don't accept reservations from June to August, and most charge more at weekends.

The Old Centre

BOB'S YOUTH HOSTEL > Nieuwezijds Voorburgwal 92 **T** 020 623 0063, **W** www.bobsyouthhostel.nl. MAP PP.34–35, POCKET MAP B11. An old favourite with backpackers, *Bob's* is a lively place with small, very basic dorm beds for €30 per person, including breakfast in the coffeeshop on the ground floor. Just a 10min walk from Amsterdam Centraal Station.

FLYING PIG DOWNTOWN Nieuwendijk 100 > **T** 020 420 6822, **W** flyingpig.nl. MAP PP.34–35, POCKET MAP C11. Clean, large and well run by ex-travellers familiar with the needs of backpackers. Free use of kitchen facilities, no curfew, there's a late-night coffeeshop next door and the hostel bar is open all night. Justifiably popular, and a very good deal, with mixed dorm beds from €31 (depending on the size of the dorm) and doubles at €50. Just a 5min walk from Centraal Station.

STAY OKAY > Stadsdoelen Kloveniersburgwal 97 **T** 020 624 6832, **W** stayokay.com. MAP PP.34–35, POCKET MAP C13. The closest to Centraal Station of the two official hostels, with clean, semi-private dorms at €40. Price includes linen, breakfast and locker, plus use of communal kitchen. The bar overlooks the canal and serves good-value if basic food, and there's a 2am curfew (though the door opens for three 15min intervals between 2am and 7am). Metro Nieuwmarkt, or trams #4, #9, #16, #24 or #25 from Centraal Station to Muntplein. See also the city's other HI hostel, the *Stay Okay Vondelpark* (see opposite), which has a greater choice of rooms.

The Grachtengordel

COCOMAMA > Westeinde 18 **T** 020 627 2454, **W** cocomamahostel.com. MAP PP.54–55, POCKET MAP E7. This relatively new hotel-hostel is excellently located, footsteps from the main museums and also from the De Pijp neighbourhood. Once a notorious old brothel, it has been painstakingly transformed into a light, welcoming space. The ground floor emphasizes the hostel vibe with its communal kitchen and sitting room and has a nice mix of small dorms, while the four private en-suite doubles on the upper levels would not be out of place in a boutique hotel, each individually designed. **Dorm beds €43, private rooms €128.**

HANS BRINKER > Kerkstraat 136–138 ⓣ 020 622 0687, ⓦ **hansbrinker.com.** MAP PP.54–55, POCKET MAP C5. Well-established and raucously popular Amsterdam hostel, with around five hundred beds. Dorms are basic and clean and beds go for €25. The facilities are good: free internet after 10pm, disco every night, and it's near to the buzz of Leidseplein too. A hostel to head for if you're out for a good time (and not too bothered about getting a solid night's sleep). Walk-in policy only. Trams #1, #2 or #5 from Centraal Station to Keizersgracht.

The Jordaan and western docklands

SHELTER JORDAN > Bloemstraat 179 ⓣ 020 624 4717, ⓦ shelterhostelamsterdam.com. MAP P.73, POCKET MAP B3. The better of Amsterdam's two Christian Shelter hostels, situated in a particularly attractive and quiet part of the Jordaan, close to the Lijnbaansgracht canal. Great-value beds in single-sex dorms (sleeping four to eighteen, from €31); rates include breakfast, sheets, shower and locker. There's a decent café downstairs. Tram #13 or #17 to Marnixstraat.

The Old Jewish Quarter and Plantage

ECOMAMA > Valkenburgerstraat 124 ⓣ **020 770 9529,** ⓦ **ecomamahotel .com.** MAP PP.82–83, POCKET MAP F4. Superb light, bright eco-hostel with green roof, water-saving system and rooms that range from "El Cheapo" twelve-bed dorms (from €30) to very stylish private en-suite doubles (€120); there's a ladies-only dorm too. Tram #9 to Mr Visserplein.

Our picks

BUDGET *Ecomama*> p.133
CENTRAL *Estherea* > p.128
BOUTIQUE *Vondel* > p.131
ROMANCE *Ambassade* > p.127
CELEBS *Dylan* > p.128
LUXURY *717* > p.128
GRUNGY *Winston* > p.127

The Museum Quarter and around

FLYING PIG UPTOWN > **Vossiusstraat 46** ⓣ **020 400 4187,** ⓦ **flyingpig.nl.** MAP P.102, POCKET MAP B6. The better of the two *Flying Pig* hostels (see p.132), facing the Vondelpark and close to the city's most important museums. Immaculate and well maintained by a staff of travellers, who understand their backpacking guests. Free use of kitchen facilities, no curfew and good tourist information. Fourteen-bed dorms start at €20 per person and there are a few two-person queensize bunks, as well as double rooms. Great value. Trams #1, #2 or #5 from Centraal Station to Leidseplein, then a short walk.

STAY OKAY VONDELPARK > **Zandpad 5** ⓣ **020 589 8996,** ⓦ **stayokay.com.** MAP P.102, POCKET MAP B6. The better of the city's two HI hostels, with a bar, restaurant, TV lounge, internet access and bike shed, plus various discount facilities for tours and museums. Dorm rates vary enormously from €36 to €45, including use of all facilities, shower, sheets and breakfast. Doubles around €120. Secure lockers and no curfew. To be sure of a place in high season you'll need to book at least two months ahead. Trams #1, #2 or #5 from Centraal Station to Leidseplein, then a 5min walk.

ELDHAFTIG
VASTBERADEN
BARMHART
AMSTERDA

ESSENTIALS

Arrival

Arriving in Amsterdam by train and plane could hardly be easier. Amsterdam's international **airport** is a quick and convenient train ride away from the city's **international train station**, which is itself just a ten-minute metro ride from the terminus for long-distance and international buses.

By air

Amsterdam's international airport, **Schiphol** (www.schiphol.nl), is located about 15km southwest of the city centre. Trains run from there to Amsterdam Centraal Station every ten minutes during the day, every hour at night (midnight–6am); the journey takes 15–20 minutes and costs €5.20 each way. Taxi fares from Schiphol to most parts of the city centre are €45–50. The Connexxion bus service (038 339 4741, schipholhotelshuttle.nl) departs from the designated bus stop outside the Arrivals Hall every thirty minutes or so from 6am to 9pm at a cost of €17 one-way, €27 return. The route varies with the needs of the passengers it picks up at the airport, but buses take about forty minutes to get from the airport to the city centre. Tickets are bought at the Connexxion desk in the Arrivals Hall.

By train

Amsterdam's **Centraal Station** (CS) has regular connections with key cities in Germany, Belgium and France, as well as all the larger towns and cities of the Netherlands. Amsterdam also has several suburban train stations, but these are principally for commuters. For all rail enquiries consult **NS** (Netherlands Railways; ns.nl).

By bus

Eurolines (eurolines.nl) long-distance, international buses arrive at Amstel Station, about 3.5km to the southeast of Centraal Station. The metro journey to Centraal Station takes about ten minutes.

City transport

Almost all of Amsterdam's leading attractions are within easy walking distance of each other. The city has a first-rate public transport system, run by **GVB** (gvb.nl). Centraal Station is the hub of the system, with trams and buses departing from outside on Stationsplein, which is also the location of a metro station and a GVB public transport information office. There's a taxi rank on Stationsplein too.

Tickets

The **OV-Chipkaart** (www.ov-chipkaart.nl) is an electronic payment card which covers the cost of travelling on all of the GVB transport system. There are two main sorts of card – rechargeable plastic cards and disposable paper cards set to a pre-determined value and length of time. Disposable cards are best for short stays. Cards are sold at the tourist office and on the city's trams and at the metro. You must scan the card when you get on and off the bus, tram, ferry or metro. A disposable *dagkaart* (day ticket), for unlimited travel, costs €7.50 for 24 hours, €12.50 for 48 hours and €17 for 72 hours. Note that the GVB tries hard to deter fare-dodging, and wherever you're travelling and at whatever time of day, there's a chance you'll have your ticket checked. If caught without a valid ticket, you risk an on-the-spot fine.

Trams, metro and buses

Trams crisscross the city: two of the most useful are #2 and #5, which link Centraal Station with Leidsestraat and the Rijksmuseum every ten minutes or so during the day. **Buses** are mainly useful for going to the outskirts, and the same applies to the **metro**, which has just three city centre stations: Centraal Station, Nieuwmarkt and Waterlooplein. Trams, buses and the metro operate daily between 6am and midnight, supplemented by a limited number of nightbuses (*nachtbussen*). All tram and bus stops display a detailed map of the network. For further details on all services, head for the main GVB information office (Mon–Fri 7am–9pm, Sat & Sun 10am–6pm; gvb.nl) on Stationsplein. Its free, English-language *Tram, Bus, Metro, Ferry Amsterdam* booklet is very helpful, and includes a free transport map.

The Canal Bus

One good way to get around Amsterdam's waterways is to take the **Canal Bus** (canal.nl). This operates on three circular routes, coloured green, red and orange, which meet at various places: at the jetty opposite Centraal Station beside Prins Hendrikkade; on the Singelgracht (opposite the Rijksmuseum), near the Leidseplein; and by the Stadhuis on Waterlooplein. There are fourteen stops in all and together they give easy access to all the major sights. Boats leave from opposite Centraal Station every half an hour or so during low season between 10am and 5.30pm (longer in high season), and a 24hr ticket for all three routes, allowing you to hop on and off as many times as you like, costs €22 per adult, €11 for children (4–11 years old). The ticket also entitles the bearer to minor discounts at several museums. Two-day passes cost €25.

Boat tours

There are several **boat tour** operators and they occupy prime pitches – the jetties near Centraal Station on Stationsplein, beside the Damrak and on Prins Hendrikkade. **Prices** are fairly uniform with a one-hour tour costing around €16 per adult, €8 per child (4–12 years old), and around €20–25 for a two-hour cruise at night. The big companies also offer more **specialized boat trips** – dinner cruises from around €60, literary cruises, and so forth. All these cruises are popular and long queues are common in the summer. One way of avoiding much of the crush is to walk down the Damrak from Centraal Station to the jetty at the near end of the Rokin, where the first-rate Reederij P. Kooij (rederijkooij.nl) – who also have a jetty beside Centraal Station – offers all the basic cruises at competitive prices.

Canal Bikes

You can rent **Canal Bikes** (canal.nl) – four-seater **pedaloes** – at four central locations: on the Singelgracht opposite the Rijksmuseum; the Prinsengracht outside the Anne Frank Huis; on Keizersgracht at Leidsestraat; and behind Leidseplein. Rental prices per person per hour are €8 (3–4 people), plus a refundable deposit of €20. They can be picked up at one location and left at any of the others; opening times are April to October daily 10am to 6pm, until 10pm in July and August.

Bicycles

The city has an excellent network of designated bicycle lanes (*fietspaden*). The needs of the cyclist take precedence over those of the

Tour operators

Gilde Amsterdam Keizersgracht 346 ⓣ 020 625 4450, ⓦ gildeamsterdam.nl. Guided walking tours of the old centre and the Jordaan by long-time – and often older – Amsterdam residents. Tours run daily except Monday; €7.50 per person. Advance reservations required.

Reederij P. Kooij on the Rokin, beside the Queen Wilhelmina statue ⓣ 020 623 3810, ⓦ rederijkooij.nl. Provides a range of cruises by day and by night, at prices that are often cheaper than the rest. Also has a (more crowded) jetty opposite Centraal Station on Stationsplein.

Yellow Bike Tours Nieuwezijds Kolk 29, off Nieuwezijds Voorburgwal ⓣ 020 620 6940, ⓦ yellowbike.nl. Three-hour guided cycling tours around the city (2 daily) that cost €25 per person, including the bike. Advance reservations required.

motorist and by law, if there's a collision, it's always the driver's fault.

Bike rental is straightforward. There are lots of **rental companies** (*fietsenverhuur*) but MacBike (ⓦ macbike.nl) is perhaps the most convenient, with three rental outlets in central Amsterdam: one at the east end of Centraal Station, a second on Waterlooplein and a third near Leidseplein at Overtoom 45. They charge €7.50 for three hours, €9.75 per day and €22 for three days for a standard bicycle; 21-speed cycles cost about half as much again. All bike rental companies ask for some type of security, usually in the form of a cash deposit (some will take credit card imprints) and/or passport.

Taxis

The centre of Amsterdam is geared up for trams and bicycles rather than cars, so **taxis** are not as much use as they are in many other cities. They are, however, plentiful: taxi ranks are all over the city centre and they can also be hailed on the street. **Fares** are metered and reasonably high, but city distances are small: the trip from Centraal Station to the Leidseplein, for example, will cost around €15, €4 more to Museumplein – and about fifteen percent more late at night.

Directory A–Z

Addresses

Addresses are written as, for example, "Kerkstr.79 II", which means the second-floor apartment at Kerkstraat 79. The ground floor is indicated by *hs* (*huis*, house) after the number; the basement is *sous* (souterrain). In some cases 1e, 2e, 3e and 4e are placed in front of street addresses; these are abbreviations for *Eerste* (first), *Tweede* (second), *Derde* (third) and *Vierde* (fourth). Many side streets take the name of the street they run off, with the addition of the word *dwars*, meaning "crossing"– for instance, Palmdwarsstraat is a side street off Palmstraat. The main Grachtengordel canals begin their numbering at Brouwersgracht and increase as they progress anticlockwise. T/O (*tegenover* or "opposite") shows that the address is a boat.

Cinema

Most of Amsterdam's commercial **cinemas** are multiplexes showing general releases, but there's also a scattering of film houses showing revival and art films and occasional retrospectives. The **Kriterion** at Roeterstraat 170 (T 020 623 1708, W kriterion.nl) is a stylish cinema close to Weesperplein metro that shows arthouse and quality commercial films, while the beautiful Art Deco cinema **The Movies**, at Haarlemmerdijk 161 (T 020 638 6016, W themovies.nl), shows independent films.

Drugs

Drugs, both hard and soft, are **illegal** in the Netherlands, though the country has long tolerated the possession (up to 30g) and consumption of small amounts of cannabis (under 5g) in designated premises (coffeeshops). In recent years there have been proposals to limit access to coffeeshops to non-Dutch citizens, though in Amsterdam this has not yet happened. Other soft drugs including magic mushrooms and "space cakes" are illegal.

Electricity

The Dutch electricity supply runs at 220V AC.British equipment needs only a plug adaptor; American apparatus requires a transformer and an adaptor.

Embassies and consulates

Australia Carnegielaan 4, 2517 KH The Hague T 070 310 8200; **Canada** Sophialaan 7, 2514 JP The Hague T 070 311 1600; **Ireland** Scheveningseweg 112, 2584 AE The Hague T 070 363 0993; **New Zealand** Eisenhowerlaan 77N, 2517 KK The Hague T 070 346 9324; **South Africa** Wassenaarseweg 40, 2596 CJ The Hague T 070 392 4501; **UK** Lange Voorhout 10, 2514 ED The Hague T 070 427 0427; **USA** Lange Voorhout 102, 2514 EJ The Hague T 070 310 2209.

LGBT Amsterdam

Amsterdam is one of the top LGBT destinations in Europe: attitudes are tolerant, bars are excellent and support groups and facilities are unequalled. The age of consent is 16. Consider timing your visit to coincide with Amsterdam Pride (W amsterdamgaypride.nl) on the first weekend of August.

Health

Your hotel or the VVV should be able to provide the address of an English-speaking doctor or dentist if you need one. Otherwise call the emergency number T 112. **Minor ailments** can be remedied at a drugstore (*drogist*). These sell non-prescription drugs as well as toiletries, tampons, condoms and the like. A pharmacy or *apotheek* (usually open Mon–Fri 9.30am–6pm, but often closed Mon mornings) also handles prescriptions; centrally located pharmacies include Dam Apotheek (Damstraat 2 020 624 4331) and Apotheek Koek, Schaeffer & Van Tijen (Vijzelgracht 19 020 623 5949).

Left luggage

Centraal Station has coin-operated luggage lockers (daily 7am–11pm) and a staffed left-luggage office (daily 7am–11pm).

Lost property

For items lost on GVB trams, buses or the metro, contact customer services on 0908 8011. For items lost on an NS train, go to the ticket office at the nearest station within five days, after which it is bundled up and sent to the Centraal Bureau Gevonden Voorwerpen (Central Lost Property Office) in Utrecht.

Mail

The privatised Dutch postal service is branded as PostNL (postnl.com), the name TNT Post. Stamps are sold at supermarkets, shops and hotels.

Money

Debit cards are now the norm, and most shops and restaurants accept these and all major credit cards. You'll find ATMs throughout the city. Bureaux de change are also scattered around town – GWK has 24-hour branches at Centraal Station and Schiphol airport.

Opening hours

The Dutch weekend fades painlessly into the working week, with many smaller shops and businesses staying closed on Monday mornings til noon. Normal opening hours are, however, Monday to Friday 8.30am/9am to 5.30/6pm and Saturday 8.30/9am to 4/5pm. Many places also open late on Thursday or Friday evenings. Sunday opening is becoming increasingly common, especially within the city centre, where many shops are now open between noon and 5pm.

Most **restaurants** are open for dinner from about 6 or 7pm, and though many close as early as 9.30pm, a few stay open past 11pm. Bars, cafés and coffeeshops are either open all day from around 10am or don't open until about 5pm; most close at 1am during the week and 2am at weekends. Nightclubs generally open their doors from 11pm to 4am during the week, though a few open every night, and some stay open until 5am at the weekend. **Museums** are usually open from Monday to Friday from 10am to 5pm and from 11am to 5pm on weekends. Galleries tend to be open from Tuesday to Sunday from noon to 5pm.

Emergency numbers

For the police, fire service and ambulance call 112.

Phones

The international phone code for the Netherlands is 31. Numbers prefixed 0800 are free; those prefixed 0900 are premium-rate – a (Dutch) message before you're connected tells you how much you will be paying for the call, and you can only call them from within the Netherlands. Phone booths are rapidly disappearing but there is a light scattering at major locations, like Centraal Station. There is good coverage for **mobile phones/cell phones** all over Amsterdam. Pre-paid SIM cards are available in telephone shops (on the Rokin and around Kalverstraat) and in some supermarkets. The Dutch phone directory is available (in Dutch) at Ⓦ www.detelefoongids.nl.

Smoking

Smoking (tobacco) is banned in many public places as well as in all restaurants, cafés and bars and even, oddly enough, in coffe shops.

Time

The Netherlands is one hour ahead of UK time and six hours ahead of EST in the USA.

Tipping

You are expected to leave a tip if you have enjoyed good service – up to around ten percent of the bill should suffice in most restaurants, while taxi drivers expect a euro or two on top of the fare.

Tourist information

Amsterdam's tourist information office, the **VVV** (pronounced "fay-fay-fay"), is straight across from the main train station entrance on Stationsplein (Mon–Sat 9am–5pm, Sun 9am–4pm; Ⓦ iamsterdam .com). They sell a range of maps and guide books. They also take in-person bookings for canal cruises and other tours, sell theatre and concert tickets, and operate a same-night/last-minute accommodation reservation service. For last-minute tickets for all things Amsterdam, there's also the online Last Minute Ticket Shop (Ⓦ lastminuteticket shop.nl)

Tourist passes

Tourist passes include the **I amsterdam City Card** (Ⓦ iamsterdam.com) which provides free and unlimited use of the city's public transport network, a complimentary canal cruise and free admission to the bulk of the city's museums and attractions. It costs €55 for one day, €65 for two consecutive days and €75 for three consecutive days. It's not a bad deal, but you have to work fairly hard to make it worthwhile.

An alternative, if you're staying for more than a couple of days, is the outstanding-value **Museumkaart** (Ⓦ museumkaart.nl), which gives free entry to almost every museum in the whole of the Netherlands for a year; it costs €60, or €33 for under-18s.

Festivals and events

STILLE OMGANG (SILENT PROCESSION)

Sun closest to March 15 www.stille-omgang.nl.

Procession by local Catholics commemorating the Miracle of Amsterdam, starting and finishing at Spui.

IMAGINE FILM FESTIVAL

Throughout April imaginefilmfestival.nl.

A mix of features and shorts hosted by The Eye (see p.96), ranging from science fiction to horror, produced by both Dutch and foreign directors. Look out for the Night of Terror event held at the Tuschinski cinema.

KONINGSDAG (KING'S DAY)

April 27

The highlight of the festival calendar: a celebration of the King's birthday, with the entire city centre given over to one massive party.

HERDENKINGSDAG (REMEMBRANCE DAY)

May 4

Wreath-laying ceremony and two-minute silence at the National Monument in Dam Square, commemorating the Dutch dead of World War II.

Public holidays

January 1 New Year's Day
Good Friday (although shops open)
Easter Sunday
Easter Monday
April 27 King's Day
May 5 Liberation Day
Ascension Day
Whit Sunday and Monday
December 25 and 26 Christmas

BEVRIJDINGSDAG (LIBERATION DAY)

May 5

The country celebrates the 1945 liberation from German occupation with bands, speeches and impromptu markets around the city.

HOLLAND FESTIVAL

Throughout June hollandfestival.nl.

The largest music, dance and drama event in the Netherlands, showcasing productions at venues around the city.

NOMADS FESTIVAL

Late June nomadsfestival.nl.

Hugely popular house music festival with its own organic market and Arabian-style chill-out lounge. Tickets sell out fast.

VONDELPARK OPEN AIR THEATRE

Mid-June to mid-Aug Fri–Sun only openluchttheater.nl.

Free theatre, dance and music performances throughout the summer, presenting anything from jazz and classical concerts through to stand-up comedy. The future existence of the theatre was uncertain at the time of writing, as its city government subsidy was under debate.

JULIDANS

First half of July www.julidans.nl.

Twelve-day festival dedicated to contemporary dance. It is held in numerous locations around the Leidseplein, with the Stadsschouwburg as its throbbing heart.

AMSTERDAM PRIDE

First weekend of Aug amsterdamgaypride.nl.

The city's LGBT community celebrates with street parties held along the Amstel, Warmoesstraat and Reguliersdwarsstraat.

GRACHTENFESTIVAL

Ten days in mid-Aug grachtenfestival.nl.
International musicians perform at over ninety classical music events at historical locations around the three main canals, as well as the River IJ.

UITMARKT

Last weekend in Aug uitmarkt.nl.
Every cultural organization in the city, from opera to theatre, advertises its forthcoming programme of events with free preview performances held around the Museumplein and Leidseplein.

OPEN MONUMENT DAY

Second weekend in Sept
openmonumentendag.nl.
Over the course of a weekend, monuments throughout the Netherlands that are normally closed or have restricted opening times, throw open their doors to the public for free.

THE JORDAAN FESTIVAL

Second or third weekend in Sept
jordaanfestival.nl.
A three-day street festival in the Jordaan. There's a commercial fair on Palmgracht, talent contests on Elandsgracht, a few street parties and a culinary fair on the Sunday afternoon at the Noordermarkt.

AMSTERDAM DANCE FESTIVAL

Late Oct amsterdam-dance-event.nl.
A five-day dance music festival, hosting hundreds of national and international DJs taking over venues across the city. Tickets for all events have to be purchased separately and tend to sell out quickly.

MUSEUM NIGHT

Sat in early Nov
museumnachtamsterdam.nl.
A great opportunity to explore Amsterdam's museums in the wee hours. Most museums are open until 2am, hosting DJ performances, workshops and concerts.

CANNABIS CUP

Late Nov hightimes.com.
Five-day festival celebrating and judging new strains, with seminars, tours and music events. Venues include several coffeeshops and the Melkweg (see p.70), which also hosts a competition to find the best cultivated seed. Single-day passes on sale at the key venues cost around €40.

PARADE OF SINT NICOLAAS

Second or third Sun in Nov
The traditional parade of *Sinterklaas* (Santa Claus) through the city on his white horse, starting from near Centraal Station where he arrives by steam boat, before parading down the Damrak towards Rembrandtplein. It all finishes in Leidseplein on the balcony of the Stadsschouwburg.

PAKJESAVOND (PRESENT EVENING)

Dec 5
Though it tends to be a private affair, Pakjesavond, rather than Christmas Day, is when Dutch kids receive their Christmas presents.

NEW YEAR'S EVE

Dec 31
Fireworks and celebrations are everywhere, and most bars and clubs stay open until morning. This might just qualify as the wildest street partying in Europe.

Chronology

1200s > Amsterdam begins to prosper.

1425 > Digging of the Singel, Amsterdam's first horseshoe-shaped canal.

1530s > Inspired by Martin Luther and subsequently Calvin, Protestantism takes root.

1555 > Fanatically Catholic Habsburg Philip II becomes king of Spain and ruler of the Low Countries, including Amsterdam. Philip prepares to bring his heretical subjects to heel.

1566 > The Protestants strike back, purging churches of their "papist" reliquaries and shrines.

1567 > Philip dispatches a huge army to the Low Countries to suppress his religious opponents; the pre-eminent Protestant leader is William the Silent, Prince William of Orange-Nassau.

1578 > Amsterdam deserts the Spanish cause and declares for William, switching from Catholicism to Calvinism at the same time.

1579 > The seven northern provinces of the Low Countries sign the Union of Utrecht, an alliance against Spain that is the first unification of the Netherlands; the signees call themselves the United Provinces. The Spanish Netherlands (now Belgium) remain under Habsburg control.

17th century > The Golden Age. Amsterdam becomes the emporium for the products of Europe as well as the East and West Indies. By the middle of the century Amsterdam's wealth is spectacular.

1613 > Enlargement of Amsterdam begins with the three great canals of the Grachtengordel.

1648 > Peace with Spain; Dutch independence is recognized.

1672 > William III of Orange becomes ruler of the United Provinces.

1770–1790 > Amsterdam is split into two opposing factions – the Orangists (supporters of the House of Orange) and the Patriots (who are pro-French).

1795 > The French army occupies the United Provinces. Many of the Dutch elite's privileges are removed.

1814 > After Napoleon's defeat at Waterloo, Frederick William of Orange-Nassau is crowned King William I of the United Kingdom of the Netherlands, incorporating both the United Provinces and the former Spanish Netherlands. The seat of government becomes Den Haag (The Hague).

1830 > The provinces of what had been the Spanish Netherlands revolt against Frederick William and establish the separate Kingdom of Belgium. Amsterdam stagnates.

1914–18 > The Netherlands remains neutral during World War I.

1940 > In World War II, the Germans overrun the Netherlands.

1941 > The Germans start rounding up and deporting the city's Jews in earnest.

1942 > Anne Frank plus family and friends hide away in the back annexe in the Prinsengracht.

1944 > Betrayal and capture of the Franks; Anne dies in Belsen concentration camp, but her father – Otto – survives the war and publishes his daughter's diary in 1947.

May 1945 > The Allies liberate Amsterdam, but many die of starvation during the hard winter of 1945-6.

1960s > Amsterdam changes from a conservative city into a hotbed of hippy happenings.

1976 > The Netherlands decriminalizes the possession of soft drugs, principally cannabis. The first dope-selling "coffeeshops" open.

Late 1970s > Amsterdam's squatter movement booms.

1984 > The squatting movement has a series of major showdowns with the police. There are mass riots.

Late 1980s > The squatter movement fades away.

1990s > Several huge redevelopment schemes are planned, most notably among the old docklands bordering the River IJ.

1992 > An El Al cargo plane crashes into Amsterdam's Bijlmermeer housing estate, killing 43 people.

2000 > The Dutch parliament repeals the laws prohibiting brothels.

2001 > The Netherlands becomes the first country in the world to recognize gay marriages.

2002 > The guilder is replaced by the Euro.

2003 > Two of Amsterdam's flagship museums, the Rijksmuseum and Stedelijk begin ambitious renovation projects that fall victim to a series of delays.

2004 > Filmmaker Theo van Gogh is shot dead in Amsterdam by Mohammed Bouyeri, a Moroccan by descent, who is enraged by van Gogh's cinematic treatment of Islam. Across the country, race relations become tense.

2007 > Amsterdam city council moves to restrict and reduce its Red Light District.

2008 > Work is halted on the underground Noord-Zuidlijn metro line, which was ill-fated from the start. Ballooning costs, tunnels filled with water and the foundations of several old houses undermined. The completion date is delayed yet again.

2008–present > Ongoing disputes concerning the city's coffeeshops, whose future looks precarious, with many Dutch dismayed by drug tourism into the Netherlands.

2013 > Queen Beatrix abdicates after 33 years on the throne and is succeeded by Prince Willem-Alexander (b.1967).

2017 > New completion date set for the troubled Noord-Zuidlijn.

Dutch

It's unlikely that you'll need to speak anything other than English while you're in Amsterdam. The following Dutch words and phrases may, however be useful; note that menus are nearly always multilingual.

Words and phrases

BASICS AND GREETINGS

yes	ja
no	nee
please	alstublieft
(no) thank you	(nee) dank u or bedankt
hello	hallo or dag
good morning	goedemorgen
good afternoon	goedemiddag
good evening	goedenavond
goodbye	tot ziens
do you speak English?	spreekt u Engels?
I don't understand	Ik begrijp het niet
women/men	vrouwen/mannen
children	kinderen

NUMBERS

0	nul
1	een
2	twee
3	drie
4	vier
5	vijf
6	zes
7	zeven
8	acht
9	negen
10	tien
11	elf
12	twaalf
13	dertien
14	veertien
15	vijftien
16	zestien
17	zeventien
18	achttien
19	negentien
20	twintig
21	een en twintig
22	twee en twintig
30	dertig
40	veertig
50	vijftig
60	zestig
70	zeventig
80	tachtig
90	negentig
100	honderd
101	honderd een
1000	duizend

Food and drink

BASICS

boter	butter
boterham/broodje	sandwich/roll
brood	bread
dranken	drinks
eieren	eggs
erwtensoep/snert	pea soup with bacon or sausage
groenten	vegetables
honing	honey
hoofdgerechten	main courses
kaas	cheese
koud	cold
nagerechten	desserts
patates/frites	chips/French fries
sla/salade	salad
smeerkaas	cheese spread
stokbrood	French bread
suiker	sugar
uitsmijter	ham or cheese with eggs on bread
vis	fish
vlees	meat
voorgerechten	starters
vruchten	fruit
warm	hot
zout	salt

MEAT AND POULTRY

biefstuk (hollandse)	steak
biefstuk (duitse)	hamburger
eend	duck
fricandeau	roast pork

fricandel	frankfurter-like sausage
gehakt	minced meat
ham	ham
kalfsvlees	veal
kalkoen	turkey
karbonade	chop
kip	chicken
lamsvlees	lamb
lever	liver
spek	bacon
worst	sausages

FISH

garnalen	prawns
haring	herring
haringsalade	herring salad
kabeljauw	cod
makreel	mackerel
mosselen	mussels
oesters	oysters
paling	eel
schelvis	haddock
schol	plaice
tong	sole
zalm	salmon

VEGETABLES

aardappelen	potatoes
bloemkool	cauliflower
bonen	beans
champignons	mushrooms
erwten	peas
hutspot	mashed potatoes and carrots
knoflook	garlic
komkommer	cucumber
prei	leek
rijst	rice
sla	salad, lettuce
uien	onions
wortelen	carrots
zuurkool	sauerkraut

COOKING TERMS

belegd	filled or topped
doorbakken	well-done
gebakken	fried/baked
gebraden	roasted
gegrild	grilled
gekookt	boiled
gerookt	smoked
gestoofd	stewed
half doorbakken	medium-done
rood	rare

SWEETS AND DESSERTS

appelgebak	apple tart or cake
gebak	pastry
IJs	ice cream
koekjes	biscuits
oliebollen	doughnuts
pannekoeken	pancakes
poffertjes	small pancakes, fritters
(slag)room	(whipped) cream
speculaas	spice and honey-flavoured biscuit
stroopwafels	waffles
taai-taai	Dutch honey cake
vla	custard

DRINKS

bessenjenever	blackcurrant gin
droog	dry
frisdranken	soft drinks
jenever	Dutch gin
karnemelk	buttermilk
koffie	coffee
koffie verkeerd	coffee with warm milk
kopstoot	beer with a jenever chaser
melk	milk
pils	Dutch beer
proost!	cheers!
sinaasappelsap	orange juice
thee	tea
vruchtensap	fruit juice
wijn (wit/rood/rosé)	wine (white/red/rosé)
vieux	Dutch brandy
zoet	sweet

SMALL PRINT

PUBLISHING INFORMATION

This fourth edition published March 2017 by **Rough Guides Ltd**
80 Strand, London WC2R 0RL
11, Community Centre, Panchsheel Park, New Delhi 110017, India
Distributed by Penguin Random House
Penguin Books Ltd, 80 Strand, London WC2R 0RL
Penguin Group (USA) 345 Hudson Street, NY 10014, USA
Penguin Group (Australia) 250 Camberwell Road, Camberwell, Victoria 3124, Australia
Penguin Group (NZ) 67 Apollo Drive, Mairangi Bay, Auckland 1310, New Zealand
Penguin Group (South Africa) Block D, Rosebank Office Park, 181 Jan Smuts Avenue, Parktown North, Gauteng, South Africa 2193
Rough Guides is represented in Canada by
DK Canada 320 Front Street West, Suite 1400, Toronto, Ontario M5V 3B6
Typeset in Minion and Din to an original design by Henry Iles and Dan May.
Printed and bound in China

156pp includes index
A catalogue record for this book is available from the British Library
ISBN 978-0-24127-030-1

1 3 5 7 9 8 6 4 2

ROUGH GUIDES CREDITS

Editor: Rachel Mills
Layout: Pradeep Thapliyal
Cartography: Ed Wright
Picture editor: Phoebe Lowndes
Photographers: Roger Norum, Natascha Sturny and Mark Thomas
Proofreader: Anita Sach
Managing editor: Monica Woods
Production: Jimmy Lao
Cover photo research: Sarah Stewart-Richardson
Editorial assistant: Aimee White
Senior DTP coordinator: Dan May
Publishing director: Georgina Dee

THE AUTHOR

Phil Lee has been writing for Rough Guides for well over twenty years and Amsterdam has long been one of his favourite cities. His other books in the series include the Netherlands, Norway, Norfolk & Suffolk, Mallorca & Menorca and Belgium & Luxembourg. He lives in Nottingham, where he was born and raised.

ACKNOWLEDGEMENTS

Phil Lee would like to thank his editor, Rachel Mills, for all her hard work and thoroughness in the preparation of this new edition of the *Pocket Rough Guide Amsterdam*. Special thanks also to Alice Tate and Amber Selby Brown of *The Hoxton*, Amsterdam, and to Eelco Douma of the *Ambassade Hotel*.

HELP US UPDATE

We've gone to a lot of effort to ensure that the fourth edition of the **Pocket Rough Guide Amsterdam** is accurate and up-to-date. However, things change – places get "discovered", opening hours are notoriously fickle, restaurants and rooms raise prices or lower standards. If you feel we've got it wrong or left something out, we'd like to know, and if you can remember the address, the price, the hours, the phone number, so much the better.

Please send your comments with the subject line "**Pocket Rough Guide Amsterdam Update**" to mail@roughguides.com. We'll credit all contributions and send a copy of the next edition (or any other Rough Guide if you prefer) for the very best emails.

READERS' UPDATES

Thanks to all the readers who took the trouble to write and email in with comments and suggestions (and apologies if we've inadvertently omitted or misspelt anyone's name): Arda Akin; Maaike Bloem; Brenda Bonte; Tessa Boon; Les Bright; Joyce Brouwer; Iacopo Dalu; Stephan Dekker; Floor van Ede; Kim Gaarthuis; Imogen Gardam; Sean Gostage; Marten Hoeksma; Helen Jackson; Jamie Jenner; Martin Jones; Lotte Keess; Dr Mary Ellen Kitler; Marianne de Kuyper; Hans Langenhuijzen; Gordon Leadbetter; Danielle Linscheer; Steve Longo; Gary Low; Mette Luiting; Colm Magee; Daniel May; Roy Messenger; Lisa Mottram; Christine van Muiswinkel; Paul Mundy; Janneke van Nunen; Shanice Ofosu; Chantelle Parsons; Jan Willem Sanderse; Duncan M Small; Peter Stoakley; Sabien Stols; Matt Thomson; Laura Tobin; Irene Vriends; Stephen Williams; Dwaze Zaken.

PHOTO CREDITS

All photos © Rough Guides except the following (Key: t-top; c-centre; b-bottom; l-left; r-right):

1 Alamy Stock Photo: Sergey Borisov
2 Alamy Stock Photo: Andreas Secci
4 4Corners: SIME / Andrea Armellin
8 Corbis: Atlantide Phototravel (b). **Greenwoods** (c)
12–13 Alamy Stock Photo: Frans Lemmens
15 Alamy Stock Photo: John Kellerman (t). **Rijksmuseum Amsterdam** (cl)
16 Rijksmuseum Amsterdam
17 Amsterdam Museum: Jeroen Oerlemans (b). **Stedelijk Museum** (cr)
19 Alamy Stock Photo: hemis.fr / MATTES René (bl); Henk Meijer (c)
24 Alamy Stock Photo: Gerald Hänel
25 Alamy Stock Photo: Iain Masterton (br). Bubbles & Wines (bl)
27 Alamy Stock Photo: Christopher Hill (cr). **Paradiso:** Bruring Media B.V. Joris Bruring (b)
29 Alamy Stock Photo: Hemis (c). **Jacob Hooy:** RenePrijden (br)
30–31 Alamy Stock Photo: Frans Lemmens
46 Alamy Stock Photo: SAGAPHOTO.COM / Patrick Forget
48 Hofje van Wijs
50 Bubbles & Wines
58 Alamy Stock Photo: Artur Bogacki
59 Robert Harding Picture Library: Michael Zegers
60 Alamy Stock Photo: SAGAPHOTO.COM / Patrick Forget
66 Alamy Stock Photo: Wiskerke
68 Alamy Stock Photo: Patrick Forget
69 Alamy Stock Photo: AA World Travel Library
70 Alamy Stock Photo: Yadid Levy
71 Melkweg
74 Corbis: Peter Langer
77 Winkel 43
84 Alamy Stock Photo: Michael Wald
87 Alamy Stock Photo: age fotostock
91 Alamy Stock Photo: Peter Horree
94 Alamy Stock Photo: Zoonar GmbH
96 Alamy Stock Photo: Peter Ptschelinzew
97 Fifteen
101 Rijksmuseum Amsterdam
103 Van Gogh Museum, Amsterdam (Vincent van Gogh Foundation): Jan-Kees Steenman
104 Stedelijk Museum: John Lewis Marshall
114 Alamy Stock Photo: imageBROKER / Hans Zaglitsch
115 De Taart Van M'n Tante
122 AWL Images: Jason Langley
124–125 The Dylan: James Stokes
134–135 Alamy Stock Photo: Robert Harding

Front cover and spine: *Canal Houses, Jordaan*
Amsterdam AWL Images: Neil Farrin
Back cover: *The Zuiderkerk bell tower*
Amsterdam AWL Images: Francesco Lacobelli

Index

Maps are marked in **bold**.

D

E

F

G

H

O

P

R

S

T

V

W

Z